FIRST FRUITS

and
The Flower of Life

NICK PRICE

Front cover illustration 'The Flower of Life' by kind permission of
Zeneteru.

Blackbirdfly Books

Published by Amazon self-publishing

1st edition

ISBN-10: 151961506X
ISBN-13: 978-1519615060

DEDICATION

'I call your fruits all the gifts of nature and grace
that God gave you at any time;
with which it is your duty to foster and feed
in this life, both bodily and spiritually,
all your brothers and sisters
through nature and through grace
in the same way as you do yourself.
The first of these gifts I call your first fruits.'

From The Letter of Private Direction,
'The Cloud of Unknowing.'

For Oliver, Saskia, and Hayley.

CONTENTS

ACKNOWLEDGMENTS

I am indebted to all those friends and colleagues who have read this manuscript over the years and have encouraged me to publish it. In the editing particularly I thank Udo Zindel and Debbie Horton. Special thanks also to WhiteEagle, a teacher of Native American ways, who wrote the following after reading it back in the summer of 1996.

This is a sacred human
His shield is painted with the colours of the Earth.

It sings its journey with haunting sweet tone
Targeting those hearts, open, ready to see.

All cannot see it
All respond to it
It is a warrior's shield
Battle-worn and rich with legend.

For some it is a mirror
For some it is a lifeline
For others a quiet cove on a sun-drenched day
With a cool breeze in which to play.

ONE

Staring at the wall

Life is not a problem to be solved
but rather a mystery to be lived.

Joseph Campbell

A friend of mine told me that she spent five years
looking at a blank white wall. She was the mistress of a man
who used her at his own convenience. She had fallen in love
with him, and her fall caused her to lose her will, and she spent
all her time in a numb oblivion waiting upon his will. He paid
for the bed, for the chair and for the table from which, head
cupped in hands, she stared at the wall for which he also paid.
It took five years for her soul to surface, and it took all her
withered strength to get up off that bed and off that chair, and

to walk out of that room.

I know how it is to be mesmerised by a blank wall, and I know how hard it is to break that spell. I was locked into a way of living, and it had become such that my life was no longer aware of itself, and I was lost in the world. The feminine feeling aspect of myself had become buried beneath the patriarchal masculine nature so dominant in our culture.

I had long since forgotten that change is the real nature in which we live, perhaps I had never remembered that in this life. So, to paraphrase Carl Jung, what I did not do willingly by choice came to me as fate.

Many traditions suggest that life spirals in seven year cycles. The sixth cycle, between the ages of thirty-five and forty-two, is seen as a period of disruption when all hell can break loose. It is a time when life tries to kill off the ego so that space can be made for the heart to open to a sense of meaning, and it is unfortunate that often the heart must be broken open. I was thirty-five in 1986, and it was then that my life reared up at me like an angry horse. Though my back was turned to it at the time, it absolutely demanded that I pay it attention. My discontent had been gnawing away at me for years, and each time it got too near to the surface I would tranquillise it with work, alcohol, sport or any other pleasurable pursuit. This discontent seemed so irrational, so self-indulgent. Why should I feel so unhappy? Didn't I have everything?

You may see straight through me, and if I could have stood outside of myself I might well have seen the obvious lie I was living, but that kind of self-awareness was not available to me back then. It was compounded by the fact that the whole world around me would tell me how lucky I was, to have it all, so how could I begin to think that it might be otherwise. My identity was a carving that had been hewn by what I had achieved, by my business reputation, by my marriage, and by my possessions. I had let myself become defined by outer appearances and qualities. I had lost touch with my soul.

I'll tell you what I had.

For years I had been considered to be the top advertising photographer in Scotland, a big fish in a small pond. I demanded the highest fees, and received many of the best commissions. Throughout the eighties I was on a roll. This was the 'me first' decade, the dog eat dog years of Thatcher and Reagan, in whose shadow, coincidentally, germinated the disease known as ME: the condition of involuntary listlessness that whispered a disempowered 'Help! What about me?' as all around shouted, 'Hey! Look at me!' But I was all right Jack, I had work, I had money, I had it all.

However I never felt secure, and I was never content. If I did a good job, the euphoria never lasted more than a few days. I was either flying high in grandiosity or, more often, crashing down in a chronic lack of self-esteem. I was highly competitive and if I was not winning I became a nervous wreck inside. The only thing that could comfort me was another win. Of course I did not show this, I did not know how, and so nobody could ever see the state I was in. Ironically, I think my insecurity often manifested itself to others as arrogance.

Once my work took me to Venice on the Orient Express, the sort of job that dreams are made of. I was the envy of all my colleagues which was something I quite enjoyed. It was October, and Venice out of season was chilly and full of echoes. The fashion model who accompanied us was only seventeen, but she was old in wisdom. I shall never forget the eerie feeling of sitting one night in a deserted and flooded St Mark's Square listening to this enchanting woman sing her grief-filled Celtic love songs. As they echoed around the damp piazza, her melodies whispered their way into me, touching awake a soul that had lain dormant too long. It was all vaguely familiar, and my heart quivered to this old memory the way the skin of an unattended drum resonates to another of the same tone being rapped by someone nearby.

In those days however, I could not contain such a rich experience, and my idea of spirit was really muddled. I would drink more spirit in an attempt to intensify the rising feelings, only to lose them as I drifted helplessly away in drunken foolishness. So that night ended with me hoping to impress the muse by trying to drop-kick one of my precious cameras into the Grand Canal. It was pretty disgraceful behaviour, but The Who was my generation and, smashed, we smashed our equipment and we couldn't care less. It was a far cry from honestly acknowledging how the laments of this Celtic angel had touched my soul. Instead of waking the next morning with a healing soul, I was bogged down with a hammering head as one of my assistants held up a bent camera in front of me, telling me how he had prevented the 'rugby ball' from ending up in the canal. In spite of all that however, the muse had knocked at my door and had re-entered my life, after which there was really no turning back.

In 1986 I had been married eleven years to Jessica, and we had three children: Oliver aged six, Saskia aged five, and Hayley aged four. They were each born with their own wonderful qualities, and I swore that I would kill anyone who did anything to harm or destroy those unique characters. Jessica worked alongside me in the business and the money was flowing to us in abundance. To others we looked like the perfect couple, and we had assistants and nannies to help us in our busy lives. By now we lived in a large six-bedroomed manse in idyllic countryside several miles west of Edinburgh, and I had a large purpose-built photographic studio which I had extended on to the artist's studio at the back of the house. It was the culmination of a goal I had set myself ten years previously.

Now I no longer had to go to work, work came to me: the mountain came to Mohammed. We had a sauna, a tennis court, and a snooker room where my clients could enjoy themselves when things got too boring in the studio. Of course we had powerful cars too, all the trappings of success. I was the busiest photographer in the country. And when I wanted to show someone who I was, it was all this that I liked them to see. My identity had become embodied in the stuff I had around me, but in fact I was lost to the world and to myself, and inside I was deeply uncomfortable.

Most Friday nights for the previous several years I would go to the pub with my two best friends, Tim and Simon. Drinking was the way most people I knew and worked with ended their week. The majority of my drinking was reserved for those Friday nights, I was a bit of a weekend binger. If I drank too much during the week I couldn't cope with the work, so I would let off steam at weekends. Most people in my business did this, in fact most of them drank all the time, it was part of the culture, and for several years the drink and the money helped to numb my discontent. We were creative people in a highly rewarded creative business, but somewhere deep down in my gut was the sickening feeling that I was prostituting myself. Whatever thrills I got from achieving some clever and wonderful image, and whatever praises I received from my peers, they never satisfied for long. At the end of the day all I was doing was helping to sell a doughnut, and my job was to stick more jam into it so that it would look more appetising. Such are the ways of advertising.

For a long time these two friends and myself had dreamed about a big trip to the Himalayas, but usually it just seemed like the drink talking. Then, one Friday evening late in 1985, Simon announced that he had taken six weeks off work the following Spring, so how about that trip to Nepal? Suddenly, subject to the blessings of our families, it all seemed very possible.

I don't want to give the impression that I was a complete drunken redneck. As a student I always had an artistic bent, I painted and wrote a lot of poetry, and I played guitar and wrote songs. I was also an extremely talented cricketer. However, I will never forget the housemaster at my public school telling me that he thought I would make a very good psychologist, or maybe a detective; he said my natural talent lay in an unusual ability to understand what makes people tick. Perhaps I should have listened to him, because it has taken me all this time to return to acknowledging this talent. Maybe this was the unique ground that I was given to till, but back then it sounded too dull and too much like hard work, and anyway it was the sixties and I wanted to be the next David Bailey.

Whilst studying photography in London in the early seventies, I became very interested in all the ideas that were flooding in from the East at that time. There were gurus everywhere. I focused in on The Divine Light Mission and Guru Maharaj Ji. My flirtation with it was fairly short-lived, though many of my friends stayed sitting at the guru's feet for quite a while. He used to give his followers something he called the Knowledge, in fact I believe he still does. I was very suspicious of this, and the same voice that told me to steer clear of LSD and the heavy drugs, told me to hold back from taking this Knowledge. I found all the Eastern ideas fascinating and attractive, but it always annoyed me that these 'wise' gurus could turn any situation around so that it suited them. They had an answer for everything, and good mirrors that they were, they seemed to reflect everything back into the faces of their disciples without being answerable themselves, and this is probably what put me off them. Often they may well have been right, but I found their sometimes slippery way of operating hard to take.

For me, the final straw came when we were to meet the young fourteen year old guru at the Divine Light ashram in north London one evening. This was a big event for all us aspirants and we were full of expectation. The place was jam-packed full and stuffily hot. For an hour or two we listened to some members of his family speak to us while he rested upstairs recovering, so we were told, from his long flight on the Divine Light jumbo jet from India that day. The anticipation and the impatience grew and grew until one of his family went upstairs to see when he'd be coming down. His relative returned alone, walked to the front of the room and announced very matter-of-fact, 'I'm afraid that Guru-ji will not be coming down to talk to you tonight because he is upstairs enjoying his new Scalextric cars!' I am sure that the Guru would advise me that had I been able to understand the profound meaning of this my life may well have turned out differently, but it was too much for my proud, independent little western self and so I moved on.

The writer who had most effect on me as a student was Hermann Hesse. His book 'Narziss and Goldmund' showed me clearly the choice I had to make at that stage of my life. There were two possible paths that seemed to start and finish in more or less the same place. One was the path of the aesthete, the monk, represented by Narziss. This was a safe life with few risks, governed by outer and inner discipline, which seemed too dull and boring to me. The other was the path of worldly experience represented by Goldmund. Goldmund came to his knowledge through plunging into all the sensations that life had on offer; he felt the highs and lows, he made mistakes, he suffered, and he found things out for himself through experience. This looked painful but exciting, and that was the path for me. So, at the age of twenty, I made a vow to myself to tread the Goldmund path.

'Siddhartha' was the other Hesse book many of us were

reading back then, and it too laid my path out before me. It seemed to embody the two polarised characters of Narziss and Goldmund in the one. As a young man Siddhartha, the intelligent son of a wealthy high caste Brahman, left the easy life to become a monk. Thus he discovered the benefits of the austere life, perfecting the arts of thinking, fasting, and waiting. However, after a few years he became dissatisfied feeling that he wanted to experience more than the limitations of the forest aesthete, so he gave that up too and went out into the world to learn about wealth, desire, and excess. These he found, but after some years he again became dissatisfied and, in mid-life, sank into despair and contemplated suicide. He was saved by a sudden memory of the spiritual unity of all things which had caused him to leave the material life behind in the first place. He ended his days as a boatman helping pilgrims to and fro across a river, metaphorically ferrying them between the material and spiritual worlds. This was the same path to which I had committed.

A few years ago, whilst staying with a friend in London, she left 'Siddhartha' by my bed. I read it again that weekend, and was quite shocked to realise how much of Siddhartha's story had literally manifested in my life in the twenty years since I had first read it. Beware the commitments you make!

These are some of the myths I have lived by, and their meaning will become more clear as I progress through my story.

So, studies done, I went out into the world and spiritually I went back to sleep again.

Our birth is but a sleep and a forgetting
The soul that rises with us, our life's star,
Hath had elsewhere its setting
And cometh from afar:
Not in entire forgetfulness,
And not in utter nakedness,
But trailing clouds of glory do we come
From God, who is our home.
Heaven lies about us in our infancy!
Shades of the prison-house begin to close
Upon the growing boy,
But He holds the light, and whence it flows,
He sees it in his joy;
The Youth, who daily farther from the East,
Must travel, still is Nature's priest, and by the vision splendid
Is on his way attended;
At length the Man perceives it die away,
And fade into the light of common day.

William Wordsworth

I spent the next fifteen years in the worldly ways of family, home building, and ambitious professional pursuits. My spiritual life was something very private, something I did not, and could not, even share with my wife. In that area of my life I was incoherent. I always kept an interesting book by my bed: Gurdjieff, Idries Shah, Lyall Watson, and for years I had been mentored by Laurens van der Post's writings. I also read my fair share of Desmond Bagley and Robert Ludlum! On Sunday nights I would always say the Lord's Prayer quietly to myself, asking Him for work and that I should do the work beautifully for the benefit of myself, my family, and my clients, and thanked Him for all I had. That was the extent of my spiritual life. Even though we lived in a manse next to an active church, the bells never drew me in on a Sunday mornings. Religion had died for me at school where chapel every day, and prayers all the time, had made me numb to communal worship.

Death back then was unknown territory to me. I had never really considered my own mortality. Even life changes, what I have come to think of as little deaths, put the fear of God into me. However, in the previous few years all three of the grandparents I had known had died. My education and upbringing had taught me to bury feelings, so much so that I felt very little affected by these deaths. I expressed no grief. Something was touched in me however, and I'm sure that these deaths acted as a catalyst for the reawakening of a conscious quest for meaning in my life.

After my grandfather's funeral, I spent some time helping sort through his stuff. There was nothing much of his that appealed to me, except one book which I took with me to read on the train back to Scotland. The book, whose title I have forgotten, quoted a piece from Ralph Waldo Emerson's essay on Self Reliance that struck deep into my slumbering soul.

There is a time in every man's education when he arrives at the conviction that envy is ignorance; that imitation is suicide; that he must take himself for better for worse as his portion; that though the wide universe is full of good, no kernel of nourishing corn can come to him but

through his toil bestowed on that plot of ground which is given him to till.
The power which resides in him is new in nature, and none but he knows
what that is which he can do, nor does he know until he has tried.

This passage rang so many warning bells for me. My professional persona was steeped in competition and the ugly falseness of envy and imitation. I literally envied and imitated other people's work, and indeed I received many of my commissions because I was so good at this. I knew that I must have something original in me but I hadn't found it yet, and at this time I had only just begun to realise that it was this sense of individual purpose and fulfilment that was missing in my life. In spite of all I had, I was unhappy, I felt very insecure, and I had very little self-respect. Unknown to me, spirit was knocking at my door.

Like a sleeper in a spy story, my spiritual self lay dormant. In such a story the aspiring spy is trained at a young age by the intelligence agencies of his mother country, and he is then planted into the mainstream establishment of some enemy society and 'put to sleep.' Over the years he becomes absorbed into that enemy culture, slowly rising in status and influence. Then when fully integrated, and maybe close to forgetting his original purpose, he is reawakened to become the master spy, thus serving his creator. This reawakening can come as a hammer blow to the head.

As spirit rises and its light begins to shine again it brings with it, in direct proportion, its shadow. The shadow that was cast by this light fell over my marriage. Just as spirit is bright, clear and stimulating, shadow is dark, murky and numbing, as it follows behind the one who thinks he is moving towards the light; and the shadow that had been stalking my marriage for a few years was in the person of a local doctor. He seemed harmless enough, making very good conversation at cocktail parties, but he was strangely attracted to the exciting life style that Jessica and I appeared to represent. I say 'strangely' because burned in my memory is a look he once gave me before I had ever even spoken to him.

I was out jogging one morning at a nearby country park, and as I crossed a road between the loch and the woods his big BMW drove slowly past me. He was looking so intensely at me that I stopped, and we seemed to enter an altered state of reality. It was a look of unveiled envy, and I saw that without doubt he wanted something from me. I realise now that what I was confronting was evil, and what it wanted was possession of all that was mine. It was not him, but it was a force that rose up between us. It was the future staring into the present. It was a moment of truth, a warning I could not really understand or heed. It was archetypal, and in a sense it was my creation: my unacknowledged light casting my unacknowledged shadow. As yet though, we were both innocent players in this drama.

For three years or so this shadow stalked me, and it grew and grew. What it seemed to want more than anything else was my wife. I felt it happening in my belly, but my head denied it. The doctor and my wife spent more and more time together, playing squash, skiing, innocent pursuits. He and his wife became our friends, and their children and our children became playmates. However, they were never really my cup of tea, as I found that our tastes and interests differed so much.

My best friends were those who had been through a similar childhood to myself and whose unspoken language I shared. He was the local moustachioed doctor's son, educated locally, who became the local moustachioed doctor. I felt that I had had to take a more risky and insecure path, which was probably born out of my early severance with home and having to adapt, from the age of seven, to the English public school system. Neither history was right or wrong, good or bad, just different.

The truth can hurt, but deception, particularly self-deception, can ultimately be far more damaging. Experience has shown me that the feeling of truth lies somewhere in the solar plexus, and is closely linked with intuition. It's as if the complex of intestines that make up the solar plexus is another brain, a brain far more attuned to the simple, and sometimes irrational truths of life. The Trobriands of New Guinea believe that the seat of memory resides in the belly and, though modern science may say otherwise, it is certainly where we feel things old and new. Perhaps it would be more correct to call it our feeling brain, the processing plant where the conscious and unconscious parts of our being coalesce.

My belly told me back then that the doctor and my wife were having an affair. My brain said, 'don't be so ridiculous!' which inhibited me from talking to Jessica about it, as I was sure I would be made to feel stupid. Then, one Sunday morning, I awoke to find Jessica already up, and I heard voices down in the kitchen. I had nothing on my feet as I went downstairs, and therefore was not heard as I approached the glass door of the kitchen. There I saw my wife and the doctor hand in hand talking intimately over a cup of coffee. I opened the door and there was a frantic scuffling of chairs as they moved apart like repelling magnets. As far as I was concerned I had discovered their affair. He left the house rapidly, and I set about confronting Jessica with the situation I had not been able to talk about for fear of sounding paranoid.

Oddly, I was relieved that my belly truths had been confirmed, I felt less paranoid, less mad. Now I had evidence, and something concrete to deal with. Consciously, for the first time in my life, I realised that I could trust my belly intuition more than my head. My future was to contain an enormous amount of pain, but this was the beginning of the gain.

Jessica denied the affair, giving a plea of 'just good friends,' and she still maintains that there was nothing going on between them back then, even though the two of them have now been living together for years. I then went up to the doctor's house to confront him. He did not deny anything, and I managed to talk the whole situation through with him. I was very civilised and British about it all and suggested politely that he should not see my wife any more. He agreed, and I believed him. Ridiculously, it ended with me shaking him by the hand and smiling as I left.

I should have hit him. I don't advocate violence, but I now have a good deal of sympathy for crimes of passion: they come from the belly, that place of truth, not from the rational 'civilised' brain. I may have done better to have stayed with my gut feelings, for it is probably true that 'all is fair in love and war.' But you live and, as you live, you learn. Snow lay on the ground, and I walked deep into the silence of a nearby wood and sat against a tree. I wanted to cry, but back then I still couldn't manage a tear. I felt numb, and foolishly thought that I had dealt with the situation, nipping it in the bud, but all I had done was drive it underground.

A month later, in high spirits, I left for Nepal.

TWO

It is solved by walking

Solvitur ambulando: it is solved by walking.

Bruce Chatwin, from 'Songlines'

Kathmandu was a total culture shock to me. If only it could be afforded, a trip to a third world country should be on the curriculum of every child's education. It was like going back five hundred years into the Middle Ages, but with the added schizoid confusion of such contemporary motifs as Michael Jackson T-shirts, Bruce Lee movies, and Pepsi-Cola. We had three days there to prepare for our trek to the high passes around the Annapurna. I spent the time wandering around as if in a dream, feeling very disconnected to this strange, ancient world. I just watched it all happen around me like some space traveller in an invisible time capsule. I think all my senses were in a state of shock, numbed by the extraordinary poverty, the filth, the foul smells and the buzzing and hassling of a mass of people scrabbling for survival on the streets.

One of my long forgotten outlets for creativity when I was a schoolboy was to write poetry and songs, it was a natural response to what was going on around me, and a way to give vent to my feelings. I had not written a poem for at least fifteen years, but suddenly I found that the only way I could respond to what I was seeing was to start writing it down as poetry. It was as if I didn't want to think about what I saw, and it was easier to let the feelings pour directly out of my heart. My intellect couldn't deal with it anyway, but my heart was beginning to break open in a process that has continued ever since.

On the first day I went out to the old city of Bhaktapur to look at the temples, but I found myself far more interested in the street life, particularly the children. I wandered around taking the occasional photograph, and then as I sat in the dusty heat idly watching a small group of three-year-olds, about the same age as my youngest daughter, I noticed one of them drop a small glass bottle that she'd been playing with. It smashed to bits on the hard ground, and at that point my western conditioning told me that her mother or father should rush out and sweep her up and away from the danger of the broken glass. I wrote this,

INFANTS IN BAKTAPUR

You stood there
I watched you
From another planet
This was your home
Not mine.

You picked up a glass jar
Turned it in your baby hands
And dropped it on the ground
Your faces were blank, learning
As it smashed.

You were filthy
The ground was filthy
The air alive with flies
And you walked over the glass
On your bare little feet.

Your world passed you by
I stayed locked in mine
Your mothers were miles away
You were alone on the streets
Living, dying, learning.

Amidst the squalor I was noticing an exquisite beauty in the people, the buildings and the landscape, which was as ironic to me as the apparent happiness and humour on their faces. How could people so poor be so light, generous, and happy? If I was down to my last five thousand pounds or went a couple of weeks without work, I became so full of anxiety that I could hardly function. Yet these people had absolutely nothing and seemed wonderfully content.

In the West we tend to gather more and more stuff around us as we get older, and we become terrified of losing what we have gained. We do not so much possess our belongings as we are possessed by them. Our concepts of happiness are often given over to, and contained by, these possessions, so that if we lose them we fear that our potential for happiness will disappear with them. So our present moment is usually spoiled by the anxiety about what we lost yesterday or what we might not have tomorrow. Could it be that one of the few advantages of having nothing is to realise that you do not necessarily disintegrate and die, and that you might be forced to live for today and find happiness in the here and now?

With the help of a good friend of mine who worked for UNICEF in Kathmandu, we found an excellent Sherpa guide whom we hired alongside four porters to carry our gear. I had two very heavy backpacks with me which contained, apart from my clothes, a lot of photographic equipment. As well as the usual gamut of 35mm equipment, I had decided to go to the trouble of taking a large format Gandolfi camera made of mahogany and brass. This proved a great boon as the people were becoming pretty tired of trekkers thrusting small cameras in their faces, and they would often run and hide or simply refuse to be photographed, whereas working at the slow pace demanded by this beautiful Victorian-style camera fascinated most people, and I would often find more folk behind the camera watching the whole performance than those in front being photographed.

It was good to get out of the city and begin our journey proper. The scenery was awesome, and in the distance there was always the allure of the high Himalayas. All this was marred somewhat by the horrendous bus journey we needed to make to Pokara where we would start our trek. The vehicle seemed to be falling apart at the seams, choking dust belching constantly through gaping holes in the rusted-out floor. Every time we went over a bump we would shoot upwards and bash our heads on the luggage racks above. It was one of those experiences that's hell at the time but is fun to tell your friends about later. The final part of the journey was made in a taxi which had only one gear and a side door missing. So after all those bone-crunching hours in dismal machines it was a blessing to begin on foot. And as the sun was setting gloriously pink behind the sacred mountain of Machapuchare, we walked away from the stifling diesel fumes and into crisp clean air, heading for the spartan accommodation of our first mountain village tea house.

As was to become my habit, I woke very early. Most of the time in the Himalayas I was ecstatically happy, and it was interesting to me how little sleep I needed in spite of all the energy I was using. In the times of anxiety and depression that I have experienced since, all I have wanted to do is sleep, which I assume is the somatic reaction to a painful life. The memory of the energy and enthusiasm I had on comparatively little sleep always serves to remind me how life can be if I am in it and enjoying it. It gives me hope, and acts now as a gauge by which I can measure my happiness.

This first morning I was awakened by the sound of ringing, not the familiar melodic peal of Anglican church bells, but the deep slow resonance of gongs from a Buddhist temple. I got up excitedly, grabbed a camera, and sought out the sound. On the outskirts of the village I came to a path running alongside the tall white wall of a temple. There in the golden dawn, some thirty metres ahead, was an old monk walking slowly towards me spinning his prayer wheel, completely absorbed in his chanting. What an image! I was in bliss, this is why I had come to the Himalayas. Immediately, with my photographer's instinct, I raised my camera to steal a picture. I use the word 'steal' for good reason, for I never thought to ask permission. This was both naive and arrogant. I instinctively acted as the photographer who wanted to capture the scene for his own ends, I was not content with merely being a part of what was happening. It was a habit born of fifteen years of professional life. But before I had a chance to take the picture, the monk sensed me and looked up. He raced towards me, prayer wheel raised like a truncheon, shouting 'Ten dollars! Ten dollars!' Now it was my turn to look a picture. In my confusion I stubbornly lifted my camera again, and this time he did hit me and screamed 'Hundred dollars! Hundred dollars!' All my illusions of a Himalayan idyll began to crumble around me as I confronted this mercenary Buddhist monk. I felt very sulky and not a little scared. The old monk stared at me severely with piecing eyes, he must have been relishing my confusion. After a long silence, he completely bamboozled me by breaking into a tumultuous belly laugh and turning on the most friendly of faces. It was all a big joke.

Such are the ways of teaching in the East. No better lesson have I had for examining what I do for a living. Indeed what right did I have to steal this picture? And what was I missing by removing myself objectively behind a camera? This was the first of many such lessons I received in the mountains. Once he had seen that I had learned my lesson, the monk and I became the best of Buddhist buddies and he let me take as many pictures as I wanted. All it had cost me was a little damaged pride.

The spectacle of the mountains and the people who inhabited them was out of this world, and to record some of it on film was irresistible. However I was confronted with the constant paradox, that amidst all this beauty, colour, and often biblical splendour, was terrible poverty, appalling sanitation, and the back-breaking way most of the people, both men and women, had to graft to make ends meet.

Nepal has one of the highest child mortality rates in the third world, and this was evident all around us. We saw many sick children. Often they would be left in the care of their slightly older siblings for the day whilst their parents were off in the fields trying to earn some money to feed the family. One morning, on the third day of our trek, I came across a young boy sitting on a wall beside the path. His right leg was horribly swollen at the knee. It looked like it might have been broken, and he was also bleeding from a small open wound. I cleaned the cut, put on some antiseptic ointment and sealed it with a plaster. The boy showed little reaction and was clearly still in shock. Nuru, our Sherpa guide, joined me and watched as the boy's father took the boy away and put him on a bed at the back of their dark shack. Nuru knew the situation well, and I heard him shouting at the boy's father. The father just shouted back, and Nuru left in disgust.

As we walked on he explained the scenario to me. He told me that because the father saw that the westerner had repaired the wound, that now the boy could be left at home to heal. This meant that the father didn't have to admit that his son's leg was probably broken, thus saving himself a three-day hike to the nearest hospital and the risk of losing some of his livestock to thieves in his absence. I don't like to think what may have come of that little boy as a result of my well-meaning actions. His is a tough world.

In the more functional families however, I would often observe something more or less lost to our culture, particularly to our middle classes. I saw how grandparents still had an important part to play in their families. It was they who looked after the infants during the day, freeing up the fitter parents to go off into the terraced paddies to work. This seemed to bring much pleasure to the children, and much joy and purpose to the lives of the old people. What a contrast to our often isolated and redundant old folk, and to our children who have learned to mock and disrespect the old.

No doubt many such ways in the East are simply born out of the need to survive, they are most likely unconscious and unpremeditated by the uneducated masses. But surely we can learn a little from their example. Somehow I think we must consciously bring this wholeness back into community life, the idea of a functioning family unity, albeit the extended family. Birth and death are so closely linked, and who better to accompany each other than the very old and the very young? I have heard it suggested (by Elisabeth Kübler-Ross MD) that we could have centres where an old person will be given their food and accommodation in exchange for caretaking a youngster for a few hours each day. What a wonderful way to bring two well-matched birds together with one stone.

It is a godsend that the only way to move and see things in the Himalayas is to walk. Walking, I discovered, is the most conducive pastime for attaining wholeness of body, mind, and spirit. The pace of our lives in the West has marginalised walking as a minority sport restricted to weekends and holidays. There aren't many people who choose to walk instead of taking the bus or jumping in the car. Walking for eight or nine hours a day gave long periods of silence and reflection, which became meditations spawned by the natural mantra of the foot-beat. There were periods of emptiness of mind when climbing seemingly endless heights, and there were periods of good conversation, debate, and humour when on more kindly gradients. Often when I found myself alone for long stretches I would sing my heart out to wild nature. The Greek word for limb is *melos* from which we get melody, and my body was singing out in celebration of the fitness I was bringing to it.

Late one afternoon we walked into what seemed like a deserted village. A brisk and chilly breeze blew loose vegetation over the stone slabs of the pathways, and scraggy hens picked at scraps in the mud. The sky was dull, and the sun was fading behind heavy cloud. It was in the sub-light of such an evening that I liked to find subjects to photograph with my big wooden camera. I quickly dumped my gear in the tea house Nuru had found for us, and went out to investigate this strange little village, taking the small camera I always carried with me in the hope of finding someone or something to photograph with the big one a little later on.

I hadn't walked far before I spotted, in a gap between some small houses, a Buddhist monastery built on a raised plateau about a quarter of a mile away. There was a little stream that seemed to lead straight to this imposing building, so I followed it. The breeze had died away, and everything was hauntingly quiet apart from the sound of the water; but as I drew nearer the monastery I became aware of another sound. It was a woman's voice singing. I followed the sound, and it seemed to come from a stone hut that spanned the stream. I have always adored the sound of a solitary female voice humming or singing even when, like this one, it is tinged with sadness. It can send me into a blissful reverie. I dare say my mother hummed a lot when I lay in the oceanic bliss of her womb. Stealthily, I approached the wooden door of the hut and peered through a gap in the weather-beaten slats.

THE MILL

She slumps cross-legged, chanting in her world
A song as sweet as the setting sun
Monochromed by flour
Grey as volcano dust

Barely defined by the spartan light
From a single window.
The ancient machine takes her sifted corn
Grinding, grinding, grinding
Clunking wooden struts and strings
Shoved by the tinkling stream
That led me there.
She may have been there always
Undisturbed, a part of the mill.
I watched from another world
An ocean of ideals.

She senses me,
She turns,
I shudder to the bone.
A tear flashes in the light
And pierces my heart.
The saddest sight I've ever seen.

Yet again I was given a salutary experience. What I was seeing from the point of view of a western idyll was eradicated by the reality of the situation. She was not at all happy in her work, her work was crushingly awful and she was miserable.

Little by little my world-views were being challenged. It was slow and it was subtle, but it was coming to me in such a way that I was able to integrate all the new things that were happening to me. I was emerging from the complacency of what had become a rather narrow existence, and beginning to feel the energies that can come with new discoveries. My evenings in the tea houses were spent reading Paul Brunton who had travelled the Himalayas in the 1930s, and he said this,

To create or to organise material energy or truth or beauty is an inner torment, which deprives the one who ventures it of the peaceful life - the life of selfishness and attachment. In order to be a good worker of the Earth, man must leave behind his tranquillity and repose not only once, but unceasingly he must know how to abandon the first forms of his skill, of his art, of his thoughts, for better ones. To stop and just enjoy them, or possess them, would be a sin against action.

The disruption which is said to go with the sixth of the seven-year cycles was taking root.

I understand now why for centuries, if not millennia, the yogis have gone up to the heights of the Himalayas to meditate and to seek the experience of Oneness. It was true for me that the higher I climbed the more in touch I felt with spirit. It wasn't just the purity of the air and the tranquillity, but I think it had something to do with the thinness of the air, the effect of altitude. Is the experience of spirit enhanced by a short supply of oxygen to the brain? Many climbers have reported such experiences, and it would tally also with the thousands of near death experiences related by those who for one reason or another have temporarily lost their supply of oxygen. For me it was not so much hallucinations or sudden insights, it was more a growing certainty of a presence, what for want of a better word I can call God. I felt closer and closer to God. My soul had taken me by the bootstraps and carried me up into the heights where I could meet with spirit.

The relation of height to spirituality is not merely metaphorical. The most spiritual people on this planet live in the highest places: so do the most spiritual flowers. I call the high and light aspects of my body spirit, and the dark and heavy aspects soul. Soul is at home in the deep shaded valleys -- heavy torpid flowers saturated with black grow there -- the rivers flow like warm syrup, they empty into huge oceans of soul. Spirit is the land of high white peaks and glittering jewel-like lakes and flowers, life is sparse and sounds travel great distances.

There is soul music, soul food, soul dancing and soul love. When the soul triumphed the herdsman came to the lamaseries, for soul is communal and loves humming in unison. But the creative soul craves spirit. Out of the jungles of the lamasery the most beautiful monks one day bid farewell to their comrades and go to make their solitary journey toward the peaks, there to mate with the cosmos.

The 14th Dalai Lama

One dawn, at 15,000 feet, I wrote,

MUKTINATH

Holy red fortresses sit solidly on hills
As ancient it seems as the gods
Guarded by the snowy rock-fast sentinels
The Himalayas.

At dawn the cock crows from the kitchen floor
The fire is lit, oats bubbling in foul pots
Guttural spasms of gobbing clear the native throats
The children warm their feet in the embers,

Outside the sun lays its first rays
On the hollows and gullies of the mountains
The shafts, emissaries of warmth
To the frozen streams and bones of the night.

Birds wheel and soar over stony paddies
Distant, distant, slowly thuds an axe
And beyond, the crumbling towers of empty villages
Bear tattered rippling flags, phantoms' foe.

And on hilltops too, these flag-bearing cairns
Embrace the valleys with their aura of protection
The spinning wheels send unknown words spiralling high
The air is full of prayer, the ground is solid.

And now the day has come, my blood is warm
I sit on and in and above the world I breathe
Will I recall this as it is and hope will ever be?
It has watered the seed, let my spirit grow.

I had expected to meet a guru at the top of a mountain who would give me instant enlightenment and tell me the secret of life. Indeed I met many holy men, particularly Hindu sadhus on pilgrimage to holy shrines in the mountains, but none of them told me anything I had not heard back in north London in the early seventies. The revelations that I did receive came from inside of myself. I seemed to be finding myself again as I connected to the earth and the people around me, and I had a new feeling of strength and wellbeing. For the first time in years I was taking pictures that were coming from my own heart, and I had begun to write poetry again from a spring deep inside myself that had not really been flowing since I was a student. I felt like a dormant seed that has just received water and begun to grow. These first stirrings of growth are often ecstatic and blissful, but beware asking *let my spirit grow* for later on this growth may become very painful.

Muktinath is a place of pilgrimage for both Hindus and Buddhists. It sits at about fifteen thousand feet in wild terrain close to the border with Tibet, beneath the high pass of Thorong La. I learned something about pilgrimage from observing a sadhu whom I followed for a couple of days whilst waiting for an opportunity to photograph him. He was a beautiful looking man with exquisite coal-black eyes. I studied him and gave him food for those two days, and then I photographed him early one morning in a forest full of ancient oak and rhododendron trees.

He had walked two thousand miles since leaving Bombay, and it had taken him two years. For food he relied totally on the charity of others, and his only belongings were his loincloth, a blanket, a cane, and a container for water. Though we could only communicate in grunts and sign language we seemed to understand each other pretty well. At one stage I asked him to keep still for a second as I was using a long exposure, but this he misunderstood and he proceeded not to budge a hair for twenty minutes. I took full advantage of his yogic stillness whilst I took all the exposures I needed. The photographs done, he trotted off ahead of us, headed for his pilgrimage goal of Muktinath, which for us was still a good three-day hike away.

Two days later with Muktinath still twenty-four hours away, there trotting back towards us, all smiles, was the sadhu. He had reached his goal, the Hindu temple of one hundred and eight fountains, made his devotions for what could have been no more than a few hours, and then about turned and begun his two year journey back to Bombay. So that is what a pilgrimage is, it is the journey. It is not so much arriving at the goal, or being lost in the future by being goal oriented (something so cherished in our efficient rate-of-knots culture), but it is the focusing that is done in each passing moment of the journey that is important, staying in the present. If one is fully prepared by such a journey, then the connection at the shrine can be made very quickly and without fuss. As the saying goes, 'it is better to travel than to arrive.'

SADHU

A sadhu from Bombay
Walked barefoot all the way
To the Temple of the Fountains
In the Himalaya mountains
By the shrines of Muktinath
Below the pass of Thorong La
His eyes as black as coal
Were windows to his soul
I have never seen a being
So much part of what I'm seeing
I didn't understand a word

And loved every word I heard
His faith and lack of fears
Had kept him these two years
His humility and smiles
Bore him two thousand miles
His dearth of all possessions
Made light of our recessions
Was the peace that he invoked
In the ganja that he smoked?

He did smoke a lot of ganja! For spiritual reasons, he said. So my poem is a little whimsical. A different poem, more focused on the true spirit of such a man living such a life, came my way some years later, and this is a coincidence I want to relate, as I think it shows the strange synchronicities that can happen as one begins to tread the path towards awareness.

Four years later, early in the Spring around the time of Lent, I was on a Greek island photographing an annual pagan festival which had grabbed my attention. One night a friend took me to the top of the island to meet a man called Manos Faltaits who ran a museum up there. We chatted into the night about Plato and the like, and all kinds of strange historical conspiracy theories Manos had developed. Towards the end of our discussions I was telling him about the holy men I had met in the Himalayas and the poems I had written. He told me that he too wrote poetry, so I asked him if he had anything translated into English that I could read. He passed me a poem which seemed to describe perfectly the life of the sadhu, and when I asked Manos when it had been written, it came as a bit of a surprise when I realised that he had written it at the same time I had met the sadhu back in 1987. I believe the more we become attuned to our dreams and the details of our waking lives, the more we get fed with these kind of synchronicities, and the more every detail in life starts to yield meaning. *The universe is a complicated web of interdependent relationships*, says the physicist Fritjof Capra, and no more so, it was becoming evident to me, than in the details of our own lives.

A CANE AND A FLASK OF WATER

A cane and a flask of water for the journey.
These are the only material needs of the wise man.
With these he will move about the country
giving advice, creating peace and harmony
teaching and healing
enhancing the spirit.

Wandering, the wise man with a cane
and flask of water for the journey.
He will move around the country.

Wherever there is ignorance,
hunger and sickness,
trouble and hatred and war and bitter passion,
there is his place,
there he will teach.

Where he is needed

he will arrive quickly,
with his cane
and a flask of water for the journey.

These are the only material needs of the wise man.

The enlightenment of love
is his real weapon.
A cane and a flask of water for the journey.
These are the only material needs of the wise man.

What your heart speaks
is the truth.
It is pure wisdom,
the richness, the power,
the honour, and the glory.

Worship from the living,
and the memory of the coming generations,
the grace of the great souls,
and the spirit of the enlightened people.

Manos Faltaits

I found that the imagery of Tolkien's Lord of the Rings was all around me as I traversed the landscape. The people who lived in the mountains were generally very happy and hospitable. They were always willing to share their food and accommodate us on the mud floors of their simple, cosy dwelling places, which were always filled with the wood smoke of their hearth and the chatter of happy travellers, both native and foreign. In stature they were small and strong, their skin etched by the wild extremes of the mountain weather. In short, and I hope without sounding patronising, they reminded me very much of Tolkien's hobbits. Everywhere we walked there were prayer stones piled like cushions on the borders of the paths, and on each were carved the repeated Sanskrit symbols of the perennial Buddhist chant *aum mani padme hum*, 'hail to the jewel in the lotus flower.' These reminded me of the runic symbols found in Tolkien's books. The side from which we approached the pass was mostly very gentle, with cosy villages like Tatopani nestling in valleys full of apple orchards or, like Ghoropani, on the side of hills amongst scorching red rhododendron trees and old forests of fabulously twisted oaks. It reminded me of Lothlorien, *the land of blossoms dreaming*, where dwelt the elf queen Galadriel, *mistress of magic, lady that dies not.*

> *Few mortal eyes have seen the light*
> *That lies there ever, long and bright*
> *Galadriel ! ...... Galadriel !*
> *Clear is the water of your well.*
>
> JRR *Tolkien*

.

On the other side of the pass the landscape was very different. It was huge, wild, and awesome, and the people there were far more self-contained and proud. It was even a little frightening, just as I had imagined the land of Mordor. Then in a tea house one evening I mentioned all this to another traveller, he looked surprised and said with authority, 'Didn't you know? Tolkien lived out here for some months and travelled all around these parts!' Now I really don't know if this is myth or fact, but it would certainly explain some of Tolkien's imagery and inspiration.

Crossing the pass of Thorong La was a moment of transition for me. I crossed over the threshold from the safety and comfort of Lothlorien (my old life), to the unknown testing grounds of Mordor (my future). It was a threshold of initiation. For us in the West long gone are the days of formalised initiation, the days when in a village culture we might have been taken by experienced elders across the abyss from youth into adulthood. Today we wait, often locked in childhood behaviour patterns well into maturity, until life throws something into our path that forces us to take stock of ourselves and to begin the processes that can take us into true adulthood, which I would define as self-responsibility and self-knowledge.

Man know thyself and thou shalt know the universe.
Temple of Apollo, at Delphi

The climb was physically very demanding, and the altitude had me constantly fighting for breath. It was like the struggle of birth where the threat of death is always a stalking presence. Nearing the top of the pass, at about eighteen thousand feet, I was managing about ten painfully slow steps before having to rest for a few of minutes and hungrily gulp down oxygen from the thin air around me, but I was relishing my solitude in the awesome mountain landscape.

I was way ahead of my party and had been alone on my ascent for quite a while when, with a rapid approach from behind, an American climber and his Sherpa guide who were perhaps more acclimatised to the altitude than I was, overtook me and, after walking on some fifty metres, sat down to rest on an outcrop of rock. They had their backs to a high peak just to the north of us.

Although we had begun our climb at three in the morning so that the freezing cold would keep us from sinking into the snow and make progress even more difficult, it was by now mid-morning and the sun had been working on the south facing slopes for some hours. As I paused for breath and looked ahead at the two men happily chatting to each other, I heard an almighty crack coming from somewhere above. Looking up to the north I saw an incredible sight, and stood transfixed by it. I guess the oxygen starvation was giving me the kind of high that the sadhu's ganja might have provoked. The whole of the side of the mountain above me had detached itself, and the snow was tumbling and gathering like a billowing cloud descending in slow motion. I stood transfixed for what seemed like minutes in awe of the grace of this beautiful sight. I wanted my two friends up ahead to share in the experience as it seemed they were unaware of it. So, in an oddly calm and detached voice, I invited them politely to take a look at what was going on behind their backs. I said, 'Avalanche.'

They took one look and ran for their lives up the scree slopes opposite to gain some height, and only then did the adrenaline rush flood me and I realised the danger I was in. I panicked and started to run too, trying to gain some height and make some distance between myself and the rapidly approaching tidal wave. Where only moments before I had been exhausted after taking only a few short steps, my adrenaline had propelled me thirty feet up a steep scree slope. My body suddenly cut out, and I collapsed rasping for breath, feeling my heart exploding in my chest. The way I felt I would have welcomed death, and I looked behind me half expecting to be engulfed and swept away by the enormous white beast; but I gasped in relief as the avalanche petered out into the gully beneath me, the one we had just vacated. It was as tame now as a gentle in-coming tide.

I glanced over at the other two whilst I fought to regain my breath. The three of us laughed nervously and threw our hands in the air thanking our good fortune. We made the prayer sign to each other, palms together in front of the heart, and mouthed 'Namaste' (the Nepalese salutation that says 'the Divine in me greets the Divine in you'), then we brushed ourselves down and continued our tramp to the top. I had never been so close to death.

Crossing this pass, and this brush with death, gave me a sense of achievement like I had never felt before. My self-esteem soared as I walked across this symbolic threshold and took my first steps into the new world on the other side.

We never enjoyed our dal bhat (the Nepalese staple diet of rice and lentils) as much as we did that night, and we slept the sleep of kings in a dilapidated, draughty sheep hut. I cannot ever remember feeling so happy as I did the next morning, it was seventh heaven. As we began walking I decided to let the whole party of friends and porters go on ahead of me so that I could amble along behind and take in the vast panoramas beneath the great Annapurna and Gangapurna mountains. The feeling of freedom was numinous as I sauntered down the path singing my heart out, absolutely at one with the world. Then I was just about to put my right foot down on the ground ahead, when something underneath it caught my eye. It was a step that I later realised marked the move into this new chapter of my life. I quickly side-stepped the object as my foot landed. It was a huge pupa which I would certainly have crushed had I not looked down. I carried on, but for some reason the image remained with me.

Late that afternoon I caught everybody else up as they descended into the village of Manang. I was escorted by several vultures, and I could hear the whoosh of their huge wings as they swooped down past my ears. Perhaps they were acknowledging the close brush with death I had had the previous day. This place was much wilder and more chaotic than the other side of the pass, and it was hard to judge how the people felt about us being there, they were far more detached and concerned with their own business. In fact they may not have cared about us at all.

MANANG

Manang wild trees blow
Prayer flags chattering
Ice rivers flow
Prayer wheels clattering.

Vultures and crows
Cruise the skies eerily
Women with hoes
Scrape the land wearily.

Children so wretched
Snottily smiling
Hold hands outstretched
Filthy, beguiling.

Processionists bang
Cymbals heavily
Archers on chang
Chanting merrily.

A Buddhist in black
Standing and thinking
Blood at his back
The day slowly sinking.

Annapurna dawn
A beautiful child
Gangapurna spawn
Live and die wild.

A change in the weather the next day brought torrential rain and, once soaked, we revelled in sploshing along through the puddles. The night was spent under a leaking corrugated roof, by a storm-swollen river, the source, in fact, of the holy

Ganges. Sleep was almost impossible because of the bullet-sized hail-stones machine-gunning the roof all night, and the thundering of the river, and the dampness of my sleeping bag. By this time, a few weeks into the trek, I was sharing my sleeping bag with quite an assortment of biting beasties, and so the night was spent in the kind of itchy contortions I had witnessed in the pupa I had almost crushed on the trail two days before. Eventually all the noises and the itching became one droning monotone and I must have dozed off.

I awoke to a piercing cock-crow, not coming from some distant hill, but a mere six inches from my ear. The shack was alive with chickens scurrying around flustered and complaining about our invasion of their home. I got out of my own invaded home, and sploshed out in search of a private spot to dig a hole for my early morning bowel movement. As I squatted and contemplated the scene in the aftermath of the storm, nearby I noticed some pigs nosing around for fodder in the mud that had been churned up by the storm. Then for some reason all the images of the last few days seemed to fall into place.

SLEEPING BAG

Like a fat pig in a sty
I lay and grunted with my fate,
The sun rose and fell,
The moon came out at night
And I locked the doors and
Tucked myself up in unneeded sleep.

But now the struggling pupa
On the road from Thorong La
Has shown me where I am.
I struggle for release from my bag
As he did on the trail
My God! I almost squashed him.

It came clear to me the next morning
Early, after the storm,
The eternal river thundering by.
My spirit is released
From that itchy cocoon
I can jump into that swollen flood
And survive.
For in those raging cataracts
There is the diminutive Aum
The All.

My life had become an uncomfortable itchy bag, and I was no longer comfortable as the sleeper in it. My way of life had become the cocoon in which I had become trapped even though, as I constantly remind myself, it was also the womb in which I incubated until I felt ready to break free of it. The realisation arose when the millions of fragmented sounds from the river, water on water, water on rock, rock on rock, the whole disjointed bedlam, suddenly became one sound. Chaos simply melted into unity, and the sound transformed into a harmonic hum ….. aaaauuummmmmmm …… the Hindus and Buddhists identify it as the sound the universe makes, what

Christians might call the Word. The Word implies a sound, and it could be that that sound was the first something to emanate from the no-thing that most religious writings call the 'unknowable' God. It is interesting that both the Hindu holy writings (the Vedas) and the Bible seem to describe this phenomenon in remarkably similar ways.

The Vedas:

In the beginning was Prajapati the Brahman (God the Creator), with whom was the Word, and the Word was verily the Supreme Brahman.

The Bible:

In the beginning was the Word, and the Word was with God, and the Word was God.

And perhaps that word or sound can be articulated as Aum.

My experience bore an uncanny resemblance to what happened in Siddhartha. Re-reading the book, it came as a shock to realise how literally I had lived out his story all these years later. As a young man Siddhartha had experienced the ascetic life of renunciation, but he felt that he was missing out on something. So, he crossed a river. On the other side he experienced the material life of the driven businessman, and discovered the deep satiations of desire and luxury, and eventually, love. After several years he tired of this too and, at mid-life, he found himself back at the river in despair, confused and suicidal. He lay on the branch of a tree, suspended over the torrents of the holy river, and contemplated rolling over into the river to put an end to it all. However, just as he was about to let go, he heard the real sound of the river for the first time. He heard the Aum and realised, in an instant, the oneness of all things.

The river, the distant ocean and the sky were all one, and Siddhartha felt part of that whole. In a flash he had recalled his connection to the One and had found a reason to live again, which was to be in service to that Wholeness. So he became the ferryman, helping pilgrims to and fro between the two worlds, the material and the spiritual.

Siddhartha had become an elder, one whose function is to have experienced life as fully as possible, and is prepared to go to the edges of death and despair until he knows himself. Then he must return into the world with this knowledge in order to help others cross the divide between childhood and adulthood, materiality and spirituality, life and death. The purpose of all this I would suggest, is that we might be released from unnecessary fear to live a full, authentic and useful life, and to move more happily towards a conscious death.

I consider myself blessed to have had these experiences. Others may be able to learn in simpler ways, but I have always had to be hit over the head by life experience in order to truly understand. How can you know whether something is true unless you have experienced it?

> *There is nothing but water in the holy wells*
> *I know, I've been swimming in those places.*
> *Listen to this:*
> *All the gods sculpted out of wood*
> *All the gods carved out of ivory*
> *They can't say a word*

I know, I've been crying out to them.
The sacred books of the East, the sacred books of the West
They're nothing but words
I know, I looked through their covers sideways one day.
What Kabir talks about is only what he has lived through
If you have not lived through something it is not true!

Kabir

THREE

Aum mane padme hum

Be not a slave of your own past,
plunge into the sublime seas,
dive deep and swim far,
so you shall come back with self respect,
with new power,
with an advanced experience
that shall explain and overlook the old.

Ralph Waldo Emerson

I could not have asked for more from my first
experience of the Himalayas. I had rediscovered myself in so
many ways, in my craft, in my physical and mental abilities, and
in my soul. And it had all come from the inside as opposed to
an outer meeting with some guru. From that distance, and
some might say a romantic distance, I had found new meaning

and love for my family and my life back home, and I was now ready to get back there. I thought I really knew myself now, but in fact the journey had only just begun.

It is important that we all find our own way on the spiritual path. In the Grail Legends, when King Arthur sent his knights out in search of the Holy Grail, each of them had first to enter a dark wood. There were no paths into the wood, each knight had to find his own way in and blaze his own trail, and it was important that he did so of his own volition. To share my journey is to share my own path, and it's clear that it is only *a* path, not *the* path.

The American Indians have a way of looking at this. They imagine a wheel or circle divided into sections like a cake. In the centre of the circle is the Great Spirit, the Creator, God, Allah, Jehovah, Yahweh, Brahman, call It what you will. Each of these slices of cake has a point, and each point meets at the centre, at God. Two slices on opposite sides of the cake, if removed from the cake, will seem like arrowheads pointing in opposite directions. Imagine these slices to be two travellers on their search through life. They pass each other on the road walking in opposite directions, each toward where their arrow is pointing (their own concept of God). One says to the other, 'Where are you headed?'

The other replies, 'Towards God.'

The first one says, 'You're headed in the wrong direction, my friend. God is that way!' As he points towards the end of his piece of cake.

The other replies, 'No you're absolutely wrong, He's that way!' Looking the other way towards where his cake is pointing. And here they might just beg to differ or worse they might choose, as history attests, to fight it out. We can easily get locked into our own narrow points of view if we don't keep the whole picture in mind.

We flew from Kathmandu to Delhi where we had a four day stop-over waiting for our flight home, and this would give us a bit of time for sight seeing and relaxation. They always say that long journeys such as these can make or break a friendship, and that is exactly what had happened although I do not intend to dwell on it here. My friendship with Tim had been thoroughly cemented by our experiences together, but both Tim and I had fallen out with Simon which was very hard on him and has remained a fairly permanent rift. So, Tim and I remained in Delhi, whilst Simon went off to Kashmir to get a break from us for a few days.

After several tussles with rickshaw drivers who had deals with guest houses of varied and often dubious repute, we found ourselves a clean place which was fairly priced a mile or so from Connaught Place, in the centre of the city. Our intention was to spend our time eating, drinking, sight-seeing, and generally having a good time. They say be careful what you eat when you return from a trek with its simple diet of dal bhat, pancakes, and sweet tea. Unfortunately we decided not to listen to such sound advice and set off in search of a feast.

We thought that we would play safe by eating at a luxurious hotel. After a couple of beers, we were shown to our table. It was like a scene out of the Raj, all potted plants, cane furniture and fans whirring overhead. So, in deference to the Raj, I ordered soup, followed by kedgeree. The Indian waiter responded in what I felt was a rather arrogant manner, so carried away was I in the ways of the Raj, and he said curtly, 'No kedgeree.' I pointed out that it was on the menu, and that therefore I should like kedgeree. He put his nose in the air and said indignantly, 'No kedgeree!' Now I was digging my heels in, and so was he. I told him again that I wanted kedgeree as it was definitely advertised on the menu. With a look that I can only understand in retrospect, which seemed to say, 'OK you arrogant English prat, I'll give you kedgeree,' the waiter turned abruptly on his heels back towards the kitchens and gave me the sideways nod of the head habitual to Indians, but without the usual smile that accompanies it. What he had not told me was that the kedgeree was deep frozen, and that it might be dangerous to cook it straight from frozen on account of the egg content. The soup was served so hot that it scalded my tongue and my throat, and the kedgeree did far worse damage but that was only to surface much later that night. Meanwhile Tim and I had an excellent evening which ended with us back at the guest house drinking coffee in the small garden with one of the other residents.

The night was warm and so was the conversation. Our new friend was a Czechoslovakian man called Ladislav who was about fifty years of age. This was of course before the collapse of the Iron Curtain. He had been working on a civil engineering contract in Iraq and, as he thought this was to be his last such contract, he had gone absent without leave with the intention of seeing as much of the world as possible before his meagre funds ran out, and he had to return behind the Iron Curtain for what he thought would be the rest of his days. For the first time on the whole trip, we found ourselves talking about spiritual matters. Although my experiences had been of an intensely spiritual nature, as yet I had not been inclined or invited to speak about any of it.

Ladislav told us how things were concerning religion in his own country. He said that the communist regime tolerated the likes of his old mother going to her Catholic church, but that his only concern was to keep out of trouble, keep his head low and to provide as best he could for his family. Yet what was happening to the younger generation worried him a lot. He said that his son's religion was materialism, which sounded a little paradoxical to my western ear. In other words, the turgid reign of communism had taught the children to only hanker after things, and that they had no concept of anything other than existential things. It sounded remarkably similar to our culture.

Ladislav had been in Delhi a little longer than us, so we asked him for his advice as to what we should go and see. He told us about the Red Fort and the flea markets, and of course the day trip to Agra to visit the Taj Mahal was a must. He also said that we should go and have a look at a fascinating building on the outskirts of New Delhi. It had only just been completed, and he said it looked quite extraordinary in it's setting on a raised piece of ground adjacent to a very poor area where people were scavenging for a living on the city's rubbish dumps. He handed me a leaflet that showed a small picture of the building. It appeared to be constructed of white marble, and was in the shape of a lotus flower. He said it was a brilliant piece of engineering. It was the temple, or House of Worship, of a religion of which I had never heard, the Baha'i Faith. I speculated that it might be some strange Hindu sect, but the leaflet told me otherwise. I strained my eyes to read the print in the soft candlelight of our cosy little garden.

It informed me that this faith originated in Persia mid way through the last century, emerging out of Islam in much the same way that Christianity had emerged from Judaism eighteen hundred years previously. Above the photograph on the back were written the twelve basic tenets of the Faith which I read aloud, as much to myself as to my friends, in the balmy warmth of the Indian night.

The Baha'i Faith:

- Recognises the unity of God and of His Prophets.
- Upholds the principles of an independent unfettered search after truth.
- Condemns all forms of superstition and prejudice.
- Teaches that the fundamental purpose of religion is to promote concord and harmony.
- That religion must go hand-in-hand with science.
- That religion constitutes the sole and ultimate basis of a peaceful and progressive society.
- Inculcates the principle of equal opportunity, rights and privileges for both sexes.
- Advocates compulsory education.
- Abolishes extremes of poverty and wealth.
- Exalts work performed in the spirit of service to the rank of worship.

- Recommends the adoption of an auxiliary international language.
- Provides the necessary agencies for the establishment and safeguarding of a permanent universal peace.

Apart from my doubts concerning the sixth tenet, I could not help emitting a whispered 'Uh-huh' after each one. It was all such common sense, and I felt a little tingle of recognition in the words as I read them. It was as if all my life experience up to that moment, particularly the recent weeks in the Himalayas, were being articulated for me in these few, simple, though far from simplistic, principles.

The first tenet alone makes so much sense. How stupid it is that some people of different religions fight over their God being the right God, or their prophet being the right prophet, thus setting one religion in conflict with another. The etymology of the word religion suggests unity, from *ligare* to bind, so *re-ligare* means to bind back, to bind again, or to reunite. So any religion that causes disunity, disharmony, or conflict is, by definition, no longer a religion. Hence my doubts about point six! This faith seemed to be saying that all prophets and religions are connected through the idea of some sort of progressive revelation from God through His prophets, who would come into the world at a given time and place, and deliver the next piece in the jigsaw for the creation of a civilised society, or more to the point perhaps, the perennial goal of a Heaven on Earth. I liked that idea, and what intrigued me about this recent so-called revelation, was that for the first time in our known history it had become possible to deliver a message to the whole world almost immediately. In past dispensations, where a message had been given to an isolated individual, tribe, or nation, there had been a long drawn out dissemination of knowledge, with all the potential distortions caused by the Chinese whispers of time.

I thanked Ladislav for the leaflet, folded it tidily, and stuck it in my back pocket, and that could have been the last of it. That night however the kedgeree began its work, and I became very ill. (When I returned to the U.K. a few days later I was diagnosed as having salmonella poisoning, most likely given to me by the quickly defrosted eggs in the kedgeree, and I also had dysentery). However the physical fitness achieved by all the trekking in addition to the euphoria of self-discovery, served to keep me on my feet.

The following morning, a Sunday, Tim was keen to go off early to take a bus tour of Delhi. Rather than waste the day in bed, and a little recovered after my night of emptying, I decided to go with him to the bus station. We left just after dawn for what turned out to be a walk of about three miles, and by the time we got there I was again feeling pretty lousy. I took one look at the bus with its lack of the kind of facilities needed for my condition, and decided to leave Tim to his day's sightseeing and to return quietly to the comfort of my own loo.

Delhi was heating up, and the streets toward the centre were beginning to swarm with people. Sunday seemed as busy as any other day. Apart from the growing pressure in my bowels, I had no need to rush, so I walked slowly, taking the time to look at all the goings-on around me. To a rickshaw driver in Delhi the sight of a westerner ambling along looking lost is like a bee finding a flower swollen with nectar, and so, like bees, they buzzed in on me. Most I managed to resist, but one man just wouldn't give up, 'Good morning sir, where is it you would like to be going? Where is it you would like to be going?'

'I'm fine, thank you, I'm enjoying the walk.

'No, no! It is very hot sir. Where is it you would like to be going?'

'Really, I'm fine thank you, I would just like to walk.'

'Very cheap sir, very cheap!'

This was not going to be easy, I was weakening and I had to think of something fast that would send this man away to seek some other honey blossom. In a flash I had a plan, and I fumbled around in my back pocket for the leaflet I had stashed there the previous night. Unfolding it, I showed him the picture of the temple and asked him to take me there. I had no intention of going there in my condition, but I thought if I was to offer him an insultingly low price for the fare after the inevitable haggling, that then he might become exasperated and leave me alone. It worked a treat. His eyes lit up when he sensed the potential fare, it was obviously a long way to the temple. 'Thirty rupees, thirty rupees,' he said excitedly.

'Three rupees,' I replied dryly.

His eyes brightened a little more, for he knew this game of bargaining well, 'Twenty-five rupees.'

Here, of course, I was supposed to up my ante so that we might settle at the real fare of around fifteen rupees.

'Three rupees,' I said again. My offer was still insultingly low, and he began to get agitated. I was not playing the game.

'Twenty rupees.'

'Three rupees.'

'Fifteen rupees.'

'Three rupees.' Now he was very angry, and he showed it by revving up the engine of his little scooter in frustration.

'Ten rupees, no less, you come!'

I had him now: 'Three rupees,' said I triumphantly and for the final time. He saw red, and with one last screaming rev and a heavy clunking of gears, he sped off down the road in a flurry of foul curses and exhaust fumes. My plan had worked, I folded the leaflet up and thanked this Baha'i Faith for its help, and once again placed it in my back pocket, thinking that it had now served its purpose. I was alone again and free to amble slowly back towards the guest house. The heat was becoming fierce and I rested for a while by some children playing cricket on a rough patch of land just off the road. With India, I share a passion for cricket. It was about an hour after the rickshaw incident when I arrived in Connaught Place, the epicentre of Delhi, where literally thousands of people, from richest to poorest, jostle for position on the pavements.

The chances of meeting the same person twice under those conditions are remote to say the least, but as I raced across one of the wide thoroughfares that led out of Connaught Place, dodging through the hooting cacophony of taxis, rickshaws, scooters and bicycles, I smacked into my friend the selfsame rickshaw driver. He looked me straight in the eye and said, 'Six rupees!'

This time he had me, I was feeling tired and sick and I had no resistance left in me. I accepted his offer, but this was not a job he would do for such a pittance himself, so he led me to one of his minions who, quite understandably, could not speak a word of English. He gave this man instructions, I presumed, to take me to the temple mentioned in the leaflet, and within moments of our confrontation I found myself speeding off in the opposite direction to the comforts of my own bed and loo. The journey seemed to take forever, and it crossed my mind that the trip was easily worth the original asking price of thirty rupees. Eventually the rickshaw came to a halt in the quiet street of a leafy suburb, but there was no temple in sight, certainly not one that resembled a huge marble lotus flower.

Once again I fumbled for the leaflet in my back pocket, and I shoved it in front of the driver pointing to the picture of the temple and then to the lack of anything remotely resembling it round about us. Meantime he sat there with his outstretched hand demanding his six rupees. Using reason was no good as neither of us understood a word the other was saying. Then, in the corner of my eye, I caught a glimpse of two people coming towards us. I turned to see a woman in her late fifties accompanied by a young Indian man. She was smiling pleasantly at me, and asked in perfect English if she could be of any help. I was very relieved, and explained to her that I was wanting to go to the Lotus Temple pictured on the leaflet, but that the driver had brought me to this place instead. She said, 'Oh! We're on our way there! Why don't you come with us in our rickshaw?' 'Why not?' I mumbled, past caring about any consequences. My fever seemed to be taking me into a strange new world of coincidences, and all I could do was accept them and watch as things unfolded before me. The woman spoke kindly to the irritated driver and placated him. Then she said to me, 'We've agreed that if you give him three rupees he will go away happy enough.' So, oddly, the journey had only cost me three rupees after all.

The three of us squeezed into their waiting rickshaw, and continued the journey towards the temple. In the presence of these two smartly dressed people I became acutely aware of my scruffy unshaven appearance which must, in addition to my feverishness, have made me seem like a madman to them. I blurted out the story of the strange series of events that had led me to their company, and the odd coincidence that they should be on their way to the same place as myself. The woman smiled wisely and said, 'The Lord works in mysterious ways!' Without giving her time to say anything else I pointed to the leaflet I still carried in my hand, and shouted out the tenets one by one so as to be heard above the wailing engine, I told these two people how much sense these principles made. It never occurred to me that they might know more about this faith than I did myself. They just smiled and let me prattle on.

We came to the very poor district on the outskirts of Delhi which Ladislav had described to us, where a lot of people had made their homes beside the city's rubbish dumps so as to scavenge a living. Beyond this, the road opened out a little and was bordered on the left by a set of brand new railings, which led to two large decorated iron gates. The gates were closed, but behind them I could see an expanse of land with impeccable pathways and flower beds, contrasting radically with the rancid surroundings. In the distance, glistening blindingly white in the harsh April sun, stood the Lotus Temple, the Baha'i House of Worship for the Indian subcontinent. All through my journey in the Himalayas I had been turning prayer wheels and chanting the Buddhist prayer *Aum mane padme hum*, hail to the jewel in the lotus, and here it was. Had I called this forth? Was this the lotus flower I had been praying for, and was the jewel, the light of God, the Atman, the Self, somewhere inside this extraordinary building?

To my surprise the men at the gates smiled a greeting and opened them up for us. The woman, whom I later learned was a very well known Baha'i called Gloria Feizi, invited me inside to be shown around by her Indian friend while she went off to do some administration. She said the temple was not due to open to the public for at least another half-hour, so I would have it entirely to myself. I began to feel a little foolish about the delirious monologue I had given them on the journey. No wonder they had smiled.

Even to my uneducated eye, this building looked like an incredible piece of architecture. I have seen the Sydney Opera House, which is an obvious comparison. Both buildings are stunning. The Opera House stands in welcome to all those who enter Sydney Harbour like a colossal sea shell, and seems to hesitate somewhere between opening and closing as it resonates to the tides of music that ebb and flow within it. The Lotus Temple sits rooted in the ground, simply opening to the heavens in perfect symmetry, and seems to invite the breath of spirit and prayer to flow freely inwards and outwards. The Opera House seems to have been built so that human spirit can speak to human spirit, and the Lotus Temple so that human spirit can speak to the Divine.

I sat out in the sun while the young Indian told me a little more about the Baha'i Faith, but the heat, now approaching forty-five degrees centigrade, was getting too much for me and I found it difficult to concentrate. I was beginning to feel extremely sick, and I told him that I would have to leave soon. He suggested that I go and sit for a while inside the temple as it was cool in there, and just get a feel for the place. I gratefully accepted. Indeed it was refreshingly cool inside, and it was not a modern air-conditioning system that made it so. There are large pools of water all around the building, and natural convection pulls in the cool air that lies over the pools and draws it up through the building in a refreshing breeze towards the crest of the lotus, making the temple a naturally cool oasis in this furnace of a climate.

I did have the place entirely to myself and I sat there in the cool silence, still a little dazed by all that had happened. I had been told that this was not a place of preaching as there are no clergy in the Faith, but that it was simply for prayer and meditation. So I prayed a little, thanking God for working in his mysterious ways, and meditating on these strange circumstances, wondering at the irony of being shown something that I might have been looking for all my life, and then having to leave it as soon as I had found it because I was feeling so ill.

I bathed in the sublime atmosphere as long as I could, but soon the sickness got the better of me again and I knew I must go. I went back out into the heat where Gloria Feizi was waiting for me. I apologised that I had to leave so soon, sharing the irony of my predicament. She gave me another of her the-Lord-works-in-mysterious-ways looks, and handed me a couple of books, one of which was her own simple introduction to the Faith, and the other a more complex book on the relationship of religion to science written by Abdu'l-Baha, the son of the founder of the Faith, in reply to questions raised by Auguste Forel, the well-known French scientist. She had sized me up me well, for both books were to get me even more intrigued by this comparatively new religion. I thanked her and shook her hand, for I had not yet learned the joys of hugging, and left.

When I got back to the guesthouse I made full use of the facilities and crashed exhausted into a deep sleep, my head swimming with the strangeness of how a badly defrosted kedgeree had lead me towards a whole new way of seeing things. In the early evening Tim returned keen to tell me where he had been that day. He described his sightseeing tour of Delhi which culminated, he said to my surprise, with a visit to the place that Ladislav had recommended to us the previous evening, the Lotus Temple. I asked him what he had seen and what he had learned. He said it was very busy, and that up to ten thousand visitors a day can pass through the place. Their guide had explained the basic ideas of the Faith, shown them the buildings, and allowed them a couple of minutes to file through the temple itself. He said it was very beautiful but that it was all over a bit too quickly. It was then that a rationale for my sickness sunk home.

If I had not been ill I would have gone on the bus with Tim, and would have been introduced to all this new stuff like an ordinary tourist. Most likely, it would have gone right over my head and I would have missed it completely. Circumstance, destiny, God or whatever, gave me a much different experience, and one to which I had to pay attention. Once again I had been given a hammer blow to the head and I had to listen. It was my illness that had taken me on such a strange little odyssey, and all that mattered at that time was for me to realise that I had found something of importance. That I couldn't stay longer mattered little, for I had the rest of my life to do all the research I needed. It was like Parsifal, the innocent fool, stumbling on the Grail Castle for the first time.

As I look back on all this now from a nine-year perspective, in my times of self-doubt, I wonder at the wisdom of it all. I think of chaos theory and the butterfly effect, i.e. that the movement of one butterfly wing in say California can have a knock on effect that might eventually radically change the whole weather pattern, contributing to a storm some time later on the opposite side of the world, in Greece say. By this I mean that I now see that if one link in my story had changed, falling out with Simon, my stubbornness, the kedgeree, the exact time I crossed the street in Connaught Place, where I am and what I am doing today might be radically different.

When I am nostalgic, tired, and weakened by this often challenging journey through life, I can become regretful and think that I might still have my marriage, my children, my house, my studio, my work, and my money, all of which I have since lost, had it not been for those events in Delhi. But would I know what I now know? Would I be able to do the work I am now able to do? Would I ever have experienced any of the incredible insights, and the moments when I am certain that *all shall be well and all manner of thing shall be well* ? I am sure that in essence all the choices along the way were my own to make but, as I had discovered, it is advisable to be acutely aware of the consequences of praying, *let my spirit grow* !

FOUR

Re-entry

To put it shortly, let that thing have its way with you
and lead you where it wishes ....
Do not interfere with it in an attempt to help it ....
You be the wood and let it be the carpenter.
You be the house and let it be the householder living in it.
Be blind for the time, and shear away all desire for knowledge,
for it will hinder you more than help you.

From 'The Cloud Of Unknowing'

It was great to get home again. I had the full Hollywood homecoming, where wife and kids are all there at the airport all rushing forward with arms outstretched, smiling and shouting 'Daddy, Daddy!' All my experiences had been of a higher nature and it surprised me, as my sexual juices rose again, to realise that I hadn't thought of sex all the time I'd been away. I mentioned this to Jessica as we began to make love later that evening, and I am not sure that she believed me.

The high was something I had to come down from as I re-entered a world that had been plugging away at the trivia of everyday life in my absence. And soon my euphoria sunk into exhaustion as I gave way to the bugs that were working away inside me, and I badly needed to rest. I began to realise too, that my time away had done nothing for my relationship, that Jessica and I were drifting apart, and that the doctor was still prowling around in the background. Neither of us could talk about it, we came from a long line of families who found communication difficult. We knew no different, and for that we suffered.

Instead we got back into work. There was tons of it around, and I was regularly making several thousand pounds a week. It was a good distraction. We had decided to send the children to private schools and our oldest child was just starting, so it seemed like we would be needing all the money I could make. But inevitably, my life began to split. At the beginning of the spiritual journey it is easy to see the material and the spiritual as opposing forces, and it can become very hard to live in the one whilst developing the other. An inner conflict starts that is very disorientating, and it was unfortunate that I was not able to articulate these feelings to my wife, and because I could not share this split with her it caused the gap between us to widen yet more.

I started to create my own room in the house where I could go to meditate and to write. I rose early every morning to meditate but I had no particular practice or system other than some breathing techniques I had learned from reading

Paul Brunton. I began to record my dreams, and dialogued more and more with myself in my journal. In Jungian terms, I was opening myself up to the shadowy stuff in my unconscious, and it was a process that was gathering impetus. It seems that spiritual awakening has a will all of its own and it will find a way to emerge into consciousness come hell or high water. You can't stop a volcano erupting. It's a waste of energy and an unnecessary cause of anxiety to reflect on chains of events that might have been different, for they were as they were, and that is as it is.

One morning, not long after my return, I woke up with the sunrise on my face and a male voice speaking in my head with an unforgettable clarity, it said simply this: *'Prepare, that ye are received!'* Hearing voices, I know, is one of the symptoms of schizophrenia but, be that as it may, I have never heard a voice inside my head so clearly before or since. It sounded very biblical, and at first I was quite frightened by what it said as it seemed to imply that I might be close to death, and that I should prepare myself for the transition. This was amplified by the fact that I was coming up to the age of thirty-eight, and I had always thought that I might die at that age, or at least that something drastic might happen. And in fact it did, because that's when Jessica left me. I think that I understood the voice correctly, but I have since realised that it can take the rest of a very long life to get prepared for the transition that is death.

If this world, this life, is a testing ground for us, a playpen where we are allowed to roam around experimenting with our free will, for this freedom to be real it follows that there must be extremes of pleasure and pain, suffering and ecstasy, excess and scarcity. The pendulum must be allowed a full swing to and fro in order for us to find a true sense of balance. An intellectual understanding of the spiritual life is a beginning, a point of contact, but the real way forward is to actually live it by incorporating all the spiritual virtues so that they become one with our nature, with no vainglory attached to their achievement.

I was needing purpose in my life, and I knew I needed help. Soon after I got back from the Himalayas a good friend of mine suggested that I go and chat to a friend of his in Glasgow, Dr. Ramona Sue. She is half Chinese, with an air of mystery and wisdom around her that I found intriguing. She lived on the edge of a run down part of Glasgow in an ordinary little house named, not surprisingly, Cathay. I met with her and we got along very well. I had no real concept, during my 'innocent fool' period back then, of counselling or psychotherapy. I simply went to see her for a cup of tea once a week, and paid her a little money for the privilege. She was very flexible with her time, and we would often spend more than a couple of hours chatting away. We talked about all kinds of interesting things such as Rosicrucianism, Alchemy, and the ideas of Carl Jung, Gurdjieff and many more besides. And of course she got me talking a lot about my upbringing: the trauma of being sent away to prep school at the age of seven, and about my relationship with my parents, particularly my father whom I feared at a core level and from whom I had inherited my inability to communicate in relationship. It was not until a few months later, when a friend gave me M. Scott Peck's 'The Road Less Travelled' that I recognised what I was doing as psychotherapy.

I read the book on the Greek island of Rhodes in the broiling summer of 1987, whilst on holiday with my family. It opened up a whole new awareness in me and heralded the next phase of my life.

Odd things started to happen. I was lying in bed early one morning with the windows flung wide open, thumbing through the pages reading about coincidences and the idea of synchronicity. It got me thinking about my experiences in Delhi, and as I ruminated on them a bird flew into the room. It was a swallow and it couldn't find its way back out again. I decided to leave it to its own devices and continued to read. The next paragraph I looked at was about significant dream symbols that had a religious connotation, and Scott Peck gave the example of a woman who had a recurring dream about a bird flying into her room!

So I learned about synchronicity with a synchronicity. It clearly showed me that something else is going on concurrent to, but hidden from, our daily existence. This something is invisible to our normal spectrum of perception, and perhaps dwells in the psychic realms outside that spectrum, or in some other parallel universe. Sometimes circumstance offers an opportunity for these worlds to merge by influencing a moment in our visible world that makes us sit up and take notice. It brings a moment of wonder and mystery, as the irrational enters our normally rational lives. Synchronicity usually raises more questions than answers, and now I just take these occurrences as a kind of affirmation from the worlds around me that I am headed in the right direction. Now, the more attention I have begun to pay to this help, the more help I seem to get, and the help comes as much from the inner world of dreams, as from the outer world of synchronicities.

That same night I had a very healing dream about my father, initiated I feel by the work I had been doing with Dr. Sue. My father had sent me to both his old schools, which had not been such a happy experience for me. At my public school there was a place us naughty boys used to meet at night, well away from the school, where we would smoke, chat, play our guitars, feel free, and generally be a little more connected to the nineteen-sixties. It was aptly named Paradise Wood, and I know that my father, also not such a good boy, went there in his day too.

We were both walking through Paradise Wood, following the pretty meandering stream that wound through it. As we left the wood I looked back over my left shoulder to see that all the beautiful old hardwood trees had been cut down and that the land, that lovely rich red soil of East Devon, had all been ploughed up. Initially I felt very sad at the demise of our secret paradise, but then I noticed something that made my spirits soar. In the troughs of the ploughed land were growing the new shoots of thousands of healthy young saplings. I pointed these out to my father, and we walked on feeling very resolved and contented together.

This dream speaks for itself and needs no interpretation. It was a gift that truly began to heal the rift in me between my father and myself. There was no need to share it literally with my father, he has his own way of dealing with things and that is his business, but it was happening anyway. We can only ever hope to change ourselves, we can't change others; but it is true that if we can work on ourselves and change of our own volition, there is a good chance that our relationship to those around us might change too.

At the same time as all this was going on I needed to follow up the events in Delhi, and when I got home I began to set about it. Through the Yellow Pages I tracked down the local Baha'is. There were very few of them, about thirty in the whole of Edinburgh, and the small fourth floor flat in which I eventually met them was in vast contrast to the drama and brilliance of the Lotus Temple in India. However, they were extremely kind and intelligent people: doctors, housewives, physicists, students, business people, unemployed, black, white, brown, yellow, and they all had one thing in common, the desire for unity. This was not the dull uniformity of communism however, this was a unity based on the celebration of our differences in culture, nationality, and opinion, a *unity in diversity*. The founder of the Faith, Baha'u'llah, said things that, to me, made simple twenty-first century common sense.

On society: *The Earth is but one country and mankind its citizens.*

On religion: *This is the changeless faith of God, eternal in the past and eternal in the future.*

And about the future: *These fruitless strifes and these pointless wars must cease, and the Most Great Peace must come.*

Now, instead of going to the pub on a Friday night, I would go and join the Baha'is at a *fireside* where we would have lively discussion and fascinating teaching in someone's living room, and I would get more of my awkward questions and doubts answered. I absorbed myself totally in the investigation of this Faith, and for two years I read virtually nothing but Baha'i books. Others might have seen this as obsessive or cultist, but for me it was a passionate investigation into truth which I practised alongside my normal life, the way others might spend time with sport or hobbies. I risked the ridicule of my peers and the alienation of my wife, but something deep inside me compelled me to carry on.

In retrospect I think it all simply made my wife resentful, not just my interest in spiritual matters, but also all the awakenings that happened to me in the Himalayas. As I worked and prepared for an exhibition of the photographic work I had done there which was to raise money for UNICEF, she did little to help or encourage me. Our relationship was slowly rotting, and I felt I was in a no-win situation where I could do nothing right from her point of view. I was bringing out the 'witch' in her, but I knew nothing about how to handle such situations back then. I was involved in a process that I am sure has happened over and over to individuals throughout history. As my spiritual interests grew and took over, my emotional world began to disintegrate in equal ratio. So whilst I ruthlessly pursued the light of my spiritual interests, my emotional problems were stacking up in the shadows, gaining a volume and a momentum that would sooner or later have to explode. I can't blame Jessica for being bemused by it all.

Eventually, the only thing between me and becoming a Baha'i was what I saw as the rather ridiculous practice of having to sign a card of declaration. I thought that it was enough for me just to wake up one morning and say, 'OK, from now on I'm a Baha'i!' In fact I thought it was a shame that this religion had to have a name at all, because names cause duality, not to mention multiplicity. This faith was about unity, but as soon as I mentioned the name to another person it sounded like I was saying, 'This is my team, what's yours called?' This is one of the terrible paradoxes of the manifest world in which we live, that in order to communicate we have to name, and to name things is to start fragmenting the unity that underlies the universe.

Christ said, *Before Abraham was, I am,* and from my point of view the *I am* was the no-thing that pre-existed the Word. The Word was the first thing to emanate from the no-thing, it was a vibration perhaps, a sound, it was the first duality. Muz Murray, a Western yogi who has done a lot of research into mantra, says that in Sanskrit the sound *wora* means truth or light, and the sound *da* means to give or to donate. So he suggests that the etymology of the word 'Word' yields the meaning: to give Truth, or to give Light. It seems, and the start of St John's gospel seems to verify it, that when we start talking about the Word, or the Truth, or the Light, we are getting pretty close to the Divine. In his book 'The White Hole in Time', Peter Russell says:

In certain circumstances it (light) appears as a wave; in others as a particle ...... From light's point of view, of course, it is neither. Since it did not travel through space and time, it needed no vehicle or mechanism of travel -- it has no need to be either wave or particle. As far as light itself is concerned, there is no duality, no paradox .... There is a realm of matter -- a realm of space, time, and separation -- the realm of sub-light speeds. And there is the realm of light, a realm in which space, time, and separation take on different properties. In one realm there are waves and particles. In the other only an energy exchange. And just as mass can never reach the speed of light, light never slows to take on the qualities of matter. They are two very separate worlds.

To my layman understanding he appears to be saying that light is relative to nothing, and that all else (matter) is relative to all else. It is a brain teaser. I have a feeling that one day soon scientists are going to discover what the mystics call God, and they are going to find out that He/She/It is unknowable, and relative to nothing. The Unified Field Theory may be the equation for God.

After the Word came the fragmentation of every thing, and every thing was given separateness by man's growing consciousness and his ability to give names to those things. Originally, it seems that in primitive cultures names were very connected with the origin of all things. The anthropologist Ted Strehlow draws light to this when he reveals that the Aranda word *tnakama* means not only 'to call by name' but also 'to trust' and 'to believe.' Naturally, naming has brought a rich sense of diversity into the psyche, allowing for a sharpening of perception. For example an Eskimo is able to decipher, and name, at least thirty varieties of snow. It is this impulse for breaking down and naming the fragments that has led us to the Age of Reason, reductionism, science, and the global consciousness of the Information Age. But these days it has lead to us taking names so much for granted that we generally only see things in isolation and we have lost the sense of their underlying unity. It's similar to the inner city children who only know milk as the white stuff that comes out of cartons, and have lost its connection to the cow. Now, what do we trust and what do we believe when we call by name?

So with this dilemma of names causing disunity in mind I had a big battle to call myself anything at all. However, I came to realise that to get anything done at all we have to use language and we have to use names, so that meant I had to dare to show my true colours and make a commitment.

The writings of Baha'u'llah were constantly telling me that *true liberty consisteth in man's submission unto My commandments,* and this indeed was a tough pill to swallow to a western mind that flowered in the sixties. But how much of our so-called liberty is an illusion, a trap? Individual independence is the modern religion, but just how independent are we? Do we not depend on the state, the government, the church, the partner, the drug, the alcohol, the TV, the coffee, the rain, the sun, the flushing loo, electricity, work, money, and on and on and on. So much of our liberty is based on a helpless, but often unconscious, codependence on all kinds of things and people. We are not so much libertines as addicts!

The more I rationalised, the harder it got to make a decision. So, as is usually the way with such serious things, my decision came not through any rational thought, but in an inspired moment. One morning just after dawn I was jogging with Sigi, our old English sheepdog, beside the loch in the country park a few miles from our home. It was springtime and there was not a breath of wind. The water was as smooth as a mirror and the only disturbance were some busy coots cutting clean v-shapes into the surface. As I jogged along I suddenly moved from this outer scene into the room where I usually met my Baha'i friends. It was like a dream, except I was fully awake. They were all sitting around me in a circle, and I was in the middle holding a declaration card. Without any forethought I saw myself signing the card, and all my friends gathered round me weeping as they hugged me. It was as simple as that, and I returned from this vision to find myself running along in floods of tears with my dog looking up at me with a concerned look in her eye. After that I knew that it would not be a problem for me to sign the card, just a matter of where and when. I decided I would continue my searching, but from within the Faith.

Like most other religions, spiritual practices, and civilised secular societies for that matter, the Baha'i Faith has its laws. One of these, and the one most pertinent to me at that time, was that Baha'is do not drink alcohol, the idea being that alcohol is a false spirit that contributes to both chronic and subtle sickness in our society and in ourselves as individuals. I had decided that I could not become a Baha'i until I had fully understood this law and was prepared to give up drinking of my own volition, rather than feeling that it was a law which I had to obey.

One chilly winter's night we had a some advertising and music business friends round for dinner, and most of them were staying the night so that they could feel free to drink as much as they liked. It developed into a long night, and after most of the others had gone off to bed, a friend and myself played a long session of snooker that went on until dawn, in the company of a large bottle of brandy. We, as a family, were supposed to go to Sunday lunch with some local friends later that morning, but I was far too groggy to make it. I liked the people and felt ashamed that I couldn't make it because of my excesses of the previous night, not to mention how Jessica and the children felt having to make excuses for me. It was the straw that broke the camel's back, and that was the day I gave up drinking.

In the Faith all dialogue about the laws is directly between the individual and God, no other Baha'i has the right or power to judge an individual for disobeying a law. In my eyes this made for self-responsibility and adult choice-making. Decisions and blame could not be appropriated anywhere other than with oneself.

Giving up alcohol was not such a difficult thing for me to do physically, it was the social pressure that made it difficult. Social drinkers need allies to drink with. Oddly, this put yet another strain on my marriage. Jessica had never drunk alcohol, and when we socialised after I had given it up, our friends suddenly became self-conscious about their own drinking, and things became a little strained. I realised that I had been carrying our social ticket in this department, and that my stopping created a new social dynamic for us that was ultimately difficult for Jessica, and contributed further to the breakdown of our marriage.

Undeterred, I got a friend to give me a declaration card, and carried it around with me for a month or so as I waited for the right moment. It came in late May when I was given an assignment down in London and I decided to combine it with a visit to the Banbury area to have a look at a Winnebago motorhome I was thinking of buying. I checked into a local hotel and realised that I was quite near the village where I had spent the first three years of my life.

After an early supper I decided I would drive over to Western-on-the-Green to see if I could find the house where we had lived more than thirty-five years previously. It was Sunday 29th May, the anniversary of the death of Baha'u'llah. I had the card with me, and thought it would be interesting to take it to the place where I had landed on this planet, my polarity as it were. I found the house easily, tiny compared to the memory of it I had carried with me since the age of three. It was a beautiful evening with a low sun breaking through dark grey cloud, which made the Spring grass glow even greener.

I wandered around the village, drawn to the bells of the village church as the locals were called into evensong. It was a seductively romantic English scenario that almost had me joining them, but I remained outside as I watched the faithful walk in. I felt that the faith I had discovered was all around me, vibrating in every atom of every thing animate and inanimate that lay round about. I no longer had any need for clergy, I was self-responsible and answerable to God alone. So I walked back to my car and as I did so it began to drizzle. I sat in the car, holding the card in front of me on my lap, it simply said that 'I accept Baha'u'llah as the Manifestation of God for this age.' I looked at the fabulous colours of nature in front of me, iridescent green on storm grey, glanced down and simply signed my name. No more than five seconds later I raised my eyes and was greeted by the most vibrant rainbow I have ever seen, a complete arc in the sky so near that I felt I was in the pot of gold. It felt like a personal affirmation from God.

And God said (to Noah), 'This is the sign of the covenant I am making between me and you and every living creature with you, a covenant for all generations to come. I have set my rainbow in the clouds, and it will be sign of the covenant between me and the earth. Whenever I bring clouds over the earth and the rainbow appears in the clouds, I will remember my covenant between me and you and all living creatures of every kind. Never again will the waters become a flood to destroy all life. Whenever the rainbow appears in the clouds, I will see it and remember the everlasting covenant between God and all living creatures of every kind on the earth.'

Gen. 9 : 12-16

FIVE

Sex in the Himalayas

Every search begins with beginners luck,
and ends with the victor's being severely tested.

Old Moorish proverb
quoted in 'The Alchemist' by Paulo Coelho

After the success of my exhibition and feeling that I had
to get away again, I prepared for another trip to the Himalayas
at the end of 1988. Although I preferred not to put any
expectations on to what might happen this time, I could not
help but hope for similar experiences. However, I have learned
that the only thing that you can expect in life is the unexpected.
Whereas, using the yoga model of the chakras, the first trip was
a heavenly crown chakra experience, the second trip was to be
much more earthbound and of the base chakras.

The first thing I wanted to do when I reached Delhi,

was to revisit the Lotus Temple. I had been a Baha'i for only a few months, and I wanted to meet some more people in the Faith. This turned out to be a chastening experience. What I discovered was that Baha'is are just like any other human beings carrying, as I do myself, their own prejudices and cultural limitations. I don't know why I expected anything else.

At the temple I met a large group of young Baha'is who were working there as volunteers. They were wonderful, energetic young people from all over the world and from all kinds of different cultural backgrounds. I had made friends with the caretakers of the temple and was being looked after by their son, Omid. Omid invited me to attend a discussion with all these young folk facilitated by an older Indian Baha'i. The debate was about hugging of all things, and what he saw as the dangers attached to social hugging. The line was that hugging was generally to be avoided as it had ambiguous sexual overtones. To me this seemed like a cultural issue. What might be acceptable, healthy and normal for someone from a liberal European country such as Holland, might be less easy and acceptable for someone from a Hindu or Muslim background. The debate got quite lively with many different attitudes, but the general consensus was that hugging is a good thing. What I found difficult however, was the facilitator's insistence that these young people should rethink their habits. As far as I could see he was just coming from the point of view of his own culture, and not opening his mind to a world-view. He was endorsing his attitude with isolated quotes from the Baha'i writings that were not being given any context. In other words he was, from my standpoint, doing something dangerous that men have done to religion over countless millennia: making one of his own prejudices sound like it was gospel.

This made me feel deeply uncomfortable as it was the first time I had been disillusioned by what a Baha'i had represented. Unfortunately, because I was a guest, I thought it better that I remain silent, which is something that I regret. I realise now that none of those present, including the facilitator and myself, carried any more authority than the others, irrespective of age, and that what really mattered in Baha'i law was the conscience of each individual. For me, this experience over what seems such a petty matter, served to ground me in the Faith and made me realise that I must walk a very practical and humble path, and above all I must walk the talk. Whatever our path, spiritual or otherwise, that is the most important thing.

Omid told me a touching story that redressed my balance a little. His family came from Persia, the country in which the Baha'i Faith originated. His grandparents were alive in the early days of the Faith. It was a terrifying time for new believers as the fundamentalist Muslims were very severe on those who chose to change their faith, the way it had been for a few Jews in Palestine two thousand years before. Thousands of Baha'is had been killed in this transition during the nineteenth century. Omid's grandfather had become a Baha'i, but his grandmother was a staunch Muslim and was horrified by her husband's conversion. There was an impasse between them that seemed without a solution. His grandfather however, simply prayed to the powers that be that they might find a way to bring his wife around to his way of thinking, or at least to tolerate him in his faith.

They had a son who became dangerously ill and looked like he might die. In her desperation his mother prayed to Baha'u'llah saying that if he was whom he said he was then he could save her son, and that if he did she would become a Baha'i. She had been regularly feeding her son on warm water sweetened with sugar. In Persia the rock salt they used looked very like the sugar, and in that particular dose that day she mistook the salt for the sugar. He almost immediately began to show signs of recovery and, realising what she had done, she continued to add rock salt and sugar to the solution, which sounds very like the present day Third World cure-all for dehydration, oral rehydration solution. In her eyes her prayer had been answered and she immediately joined her husband as a Baha'i.

Omid also told me a dream. At night his family, alone in the grounds as the caretakers of the House of Worship, slept in their flat directly below the marble lotus petals, surely a very powerful place for the psyche of a young believer to germinate, and for the unconscious to emerge in dream.

I was in a desert doing some work with solar energy, and there were some spirits there with me. Then the spirits were outside the railings of the Lotus Temple, and I was watching them from the inside. They were the spirits of the resurrected dead, and they all wanted to get in, but they told me that they could not become Baha'is in the spirit world if they had not died as Baha'is, and therefore could not gain entry.

Who knows what or when the day of resurrection is, or

if indeed there will be such a time, but this dream seems to carry an urgent message that belongs as much to the collective unconscious as to Omid's personal unconscious. Baha'is do not proselytise, but they like to talk about Baha'u'llah if invited. 'Baha'u'llah' translates literally as The Glory of God, and my understanding is that any person who is bathed in the Glory of the light of God, whatever name they choose to give to it and whatever they like to call themselves, is Baha'i meaning Glory.

BAHA'U'LLAH
THE NEW DAY

The light of dawn
First touches the skies
Of the East
The Sun still below
The horizon.

The light grows
In beauty
And in strength
While still most people
Lie asleep.

A few sit and gaze
In wonder
Meditating
Upon this dawn
Which they await.

And the Sun slowly rises
Above the horizon
Joy and purity
A perfect orb
In the East.

At its rising
Clouds vie with the Sun
Trying to hide
And destroy
Its Heavenly powers.

But the skies
Are full of Glory.
The rays reach forward
Stretching across the world
To the West.

As the light spills
Across the hemisphere
The people waken
And bathe in the aura
Of the New Day.

A little wiser I set off on Royal Nepal Airlines to Kathmandu. This time there was no feeling of culture shock, and I acclimatised immediately to the familiar sights and smells. I felt at home. Tim and his new wife Dorota were going to meet me ten days later in Kathmandu when we hoped to make the trek to Everest base camp. In the meantime George McBean, the friend who works for UNICEF, and myself were going to spend a week over in western Nepal photographing the lokta cutters. Lokta is the wood from which the Nepalese make the pulp for their very beautiful paper products, now a good source of income for a whole chain of people from the cutters high up in the mountain villages, to the workers in the small factories down in the Kathmandu valley. Myself and an American photographer spent an interesting week recording this whole chain.

In the time I had in Kathmandu I was to arrange the trek with Nuru's wife Shanti. Shanti was going to act as our guide up as far as Namche Bazaar, where we would meet up with Nuru who would take us the rest of the way to his Sherpa homelands in the Khumbu region of Everest. I had met Shanti briefly on the last visit in their tiny room in a very rough district, mice and cockroaches scuttling around on the mud floor under the spartan furniture. I had been stunned by her natural beauty: luscious black hair, huge brown eyes, delicate features and a lithe slim body underneath her red sari.

I tracked her down through Nuru's friends at the Sherpa Co-op in the Patan district of the city. The family had moved to a slightly bigger room in a better part of town, still very rough by our standards, but she was very proud of it. Nuru was off on a climbing expedition, and Shanti was alone with her little daughter Sanina. She was still just as beautiful, and it felt very exciting to be alone with her, though I didn't for a moment consider acting on my feelings. She had made most of the arrangements for our trek, and we agreed to meet in a few days time to make the bus journey to Jiri where we would begin walking.

My relationship with Jessica had deteriorated such that we were hardly ever making love any more, but in my way I was still trying to keep the relationship alive. I still felt loyal to her, I still felt I loved her, and had the added pressure now of walking the talk as a Baha'i. Like most other spiritual traditions, Baha'is teach the sanctity of marriage. I understood the wisdom of this intellectually, but I still had to live it, and be tested on it.

In the days I was waiting for Tim and Dorota, I made an appointment to see a famous palm reader, or hand analyst as he called himself. Llalji had a series of rooms opposite the palace, quite smart by Kathmandu standards. I spent about four hours with him. He spent the first hour just looking at my hands and meditating, then he made hand prints and made detailed markings on both the prints and my hands which I later realised represented years and periods of time. Then, with his eyes shut, he spoke for about an hour and a half with great precision and formality. This he taped. Only at the end was I allowed to speak and ask questions. The whole process seemed impressively scientific, though paradoxically most of the information seemed to emerge from his intuitive meditation.

He talked not so much of events in my life as of traits of character, and he was uncannily accurate. He talked about my crippling shyness as a child, and how I emerged from that problem over the years. He talked about the conflict between my poetic self, and the more extrovert self that was able to do things in the world. He stressed the importance that I should find a way of balancing these material and spiritual dualities.

'It is as if when you are at work you want to be at play, and when you are playing you want to be working.' How right he was. And he continued in his engaging Indian accent.

'Balance is like when you sit down. You don't put all your weight on to one buttock or the other buttock. No! You balance the weight evenly between your two buttocks! And when you look at things, you do not just look with your right eyeball or your left eyeball, you naturally balance your vision and get things in perspective with both eyeballs. So it is with balancing your spiritual and material life.' I took his point, and asked him to expand upon this quest for balance.

'In searching for balance, that very act of searching will lead to imbalance. The point is that balance is a state of attaining not a state of searching. Searching will always be directed toward a goal and anything which becomes polarised in that way will topple the balance and will bring about imbalance. Then you move on again and swing toward the other extreme and that too leads to imbalance, and on and on the process goes. Whereas the point is to attain balance, not to search for balance.'

'How do I attain balance without searching for it?'

'The thirst is inward, not so much outward. You can focus in on balance in your daily living, even in the slight matters, like sitting or standing. You ask yourself if both buttocks or both feet carry an even distribution of weight fifty-fifty. The criterion is not that you fulfil an outer technicality of weights and measures, but that it feels fifty-fifty from the inside. The outer search will be toward the correctness of the outward balance, and the outward balance will prove to not be inwardly fulfilling, for the thirst comes from inside. So, outwardly you must go on searching and doing whatever you want to do, and it will be an alleyway down which you can channel your own temperamental restlessness, but that will not be a real authentic solution. Fulfilment of the inner thirst lies in attaining the balance, and that will be the outcome of balance being felt by you on the inside and not in trying to create balance in any outer way. The moment you try to bring about balance by interfering with the process you will disturb the potential for attaining balance. It is existential and experiential, you cannot impose it in any outer way. Wait, and balance will come automatically.'

'Can you give me an example?'

'It's like somebody who is so fulfilled in hearing his own inner music, and yet by and by in a state of wakefulness he tries to reproduce that music on an instrument, but it emerges as crude and coarse in comparison to the inner sound. Yet it is an urge in him that needs to be expressed. Authentic balance originates from within, its outer expression always takes on a cruder form and its source cannot be found there on the outside: appeasing hunger with a candy is not the real answer.'

'This sounds like yoga,' I said.

'Yes, but there are two fundamentally different approaches to yoga, the objective and the subjective. The yoga that imposes an outward discipline on the correctness and duration of a posture, this is objective yoga. Subjective yoga has nothing to do with the correctness of the posture as visible outwardly, but it emphasises the smoothness of the feeling inwardly of doing the posture. This yoga moves more towards spiritual awareness, inner fulfillment, and synchronicity of the system. The yoga of correct posture is healthy and beneficial physiologically and mentally, but it is a much more crude tool with which to bring about synchronicity of the system, which is an internal feeling that has to come from the core of your being.'

'So, once the inner balance is achieved it may manifest itself outwardly.'

'Yes, sure enough! Then all things fall into order. There is no need to force or impose anything. You just start working along the lines you want to work. I mean that it is like when you are trying to forget a person who you do not want to be with any longer, but focusing on them and the need to forget them only causes you to remember them! No, rather focus on the person whom you would rather be with, then automatically you will erase the memory of the other person! So, remain focused on what you want and automatically the whole thing balances itself, to the extent that it even manifests outwardly, and when it does you don't even realise that things are balanced. Only through imbalance do you notice the state of balance. It is very difficult to realise things when they are in balance. When your thumb is healthy and perfect you forget that it exists almost twenty-four hours a day, but when it is broken and it hurts you remember it all day long!'

'So when we are balanced through inner awareness, we will not think about life, we'll just be in it and do it.'

'Yes, that's right!'

'And if I look at my character traits and accept them,

that's half the battle.'

'Not accept them, channelise them. Accepting suggests a reluctant, negative attitude. This is not the right approach. The point is 'this is so, now how can I channel it?' It is like Nepal, it has mountains and forests. Instead of saying, 'We don't have plains and good land for agriculture so we'll have to take the mountains down, no, we have to take the attitude that this is so, now how best can we channelise what we have got.'

'Yes, I see what you're saying. And with this attitude the spiritual and the material will work together?'

'Well, almost! The material is only in your waking hours, but the spiritual has to be twenty-four hours, day and night.'

It has taken me eight years to begin to live and understand the teaching in that conversation.

He said that in relationship I was best suited to a woman who was happy to stay in the background and who was aligned to my poetic self, and it would be better that she did not share any of my business life. This sounded very Hindu to me, and was the antithesis of Jessica. But I have to admit that there was something in the idea that appealed to me, and put me in mind of Shanti. He also made the revelation that I was not well suited to getting on with young children. My children at the time were four, six, and seven, and the idea of this remark upset me terribly. I do not think that I was a bad father, and at the time I was certainly a good provider, but Jessica often made me feel like I was a bad father, particularly in the way she sometimes talked to her friends about me. So, perhaps there was a element of truth in what she said after all.

The bus trip to Jiri was twelve hours of purgatory, but

the journey was made tolerable and even exciting because I was sitting next to Shanti, and the careering of the bus on the uneven road surfaces meant that I had a lot of body contact with her. I pretended not to notice, and not for a moment did I consider that she might be enjoying it too. For this reason I was a little disappointed when we arrived in Jiri, which reminded me of a rather dilapidated Alpine village, and my excuse for physical contact had ended.

We spent a uncomfortable night in Jiri, with the constant disturbance throughout the early hours of the morning of the buses blowing their horns to warn passengers of their immanent departure. We got out of that village as fast as we could, and began our climb into the mountains. We were joined almost immediately by a very tall Canadian doctor and his travelling companion Joel, a film student, and they stayed with us for most of the trek.

The next evening we were in Bhandar, a much more beautiful place. However the room we stayed in that night was crammed full of other travellers and we were all sleeping head to head and feet to feet. I was head to head with Shanti, and I could smell her smell and feel her breathing. Still I had no reason to believe that she was in any way attracted to me. She was the wife of a good friend of mine, and I imagined the Hindus to be very strict in their marital and sexual mores.

However, during the night I was awakened several times by Shanti's hand which I imagined had strayed in her sleep and was brushing against my hair. As it began to happen more often I realised that she was awake and was doing it on purpose. Vital juices flooded my being as desire rose uncontrollably in me. Oblivious to all the other bodies in close proximity, I moved over towards Shanti and kissed her passionately. Her small breasts heaved, and I explored her body lost in the passion. She was completely mine until my fingers reached forwards around from her buttocks, then she gently pulled my hand away whilst still holding on to our fervent kiss. It was this move that brought me to my senses, and suddenly waking up to what I was doing I pulled myself away from her, making a sign that we must stop. I got up, found my way outside in the half-light of a cloudy dawn, and went for a long walk. Shanti means Peace, and I felt anything but peaceful. I was confused and on fire, but I was feeling very alive.

Our bellies full of good tsampa (porridge) we started walking again. I drew alongside Shanti and explained to her as best I could, considering our language barrier, that what had happened the previous night was not such a good idea, that Nuru was my best friend, and that I too was married. She smiled beautifully and seemed to understand, and so I thought that I had successfully nipped it all in the bud.

I was much fitter than all the others because I had already had the hard trek with George in western Nepal a week or so earlier. So I steamed on ahead of all the others, which allowed me time to myself to consider the situation. I knew my marriage was in big trouble but I really wanted to put in the effort to make it work, and that meant being faithful to it even when I was half way around the world and completely out of sight. If I was unfaithful I would be deceiving myself as much as Jessica.

'tis in ourselves that we are thus or thus.

William Shakespeare

I had sailed close to the wind with Shanti the previous night, but now I decided to stay clear of temptation. And I wondered how Jessica was doing back home with her temptations.

The spiritual path is full of tests, and the further you travel along the path the thicker and faster those tests seem to come. It is as if the angels laugh when they hear you say, 'Oh yes! I've been there, I've dealt with that, I've passed that test,' almost immediately they respond with, 'So you really think so do you? See what you can make of this then!' And immediately you get an even harder test in the same arena.

About mid-afternoon I arrived at a spectacular location called Junbesi. It was a small gathering of whitewashed buildings which sat at the top of a high valley looking back down over a neat little Buddhist stupa towards the now not so distant mountain peaks to the west, and what promised to be an enchanting sunset. I didn't know how far ahead of the others I was, but I thought that we'd all have had enough walking for the day by the time they arrived, so I went about finding the owner of these buildings to see if we could spend the night there.

Nearby on the terraced plateau of a rice paddy, a man was working at the plough with his yak. I asked him if we could spend the night there and my sign language obviously worked, as he called his wife who showed me around and promised us a good meal and hot water to wash. The accommodation was much more luxurious than usual in that there were three separate partitioned rooms for us to sleep in, with plenty of space for the porters with the farmer and his wife next door. Each room had two bunks, and by simple deduction I soon realised that I would have to share one of these private spaces with Shanti, as my other four friends were coupled. But the setting and the promise of a good meal and a good wash were too tempting and so I booked the place for the night.

I sat looking out over the beautiful scene and meditated as I waited for the others to arrive. It was another two hours before they had all made it, by which time I felt supremely settled and content. The woman had boiled up plenty of water ready for us and had begun to cook the evening meal. So one after the other we did our ablutions from the bowl of warm water. Often we could go days without washing, and we would all happily stink together, but it was a great feeling to be clean again.

One of my greatest pleasures in the mountains was to watch 'une femme à sa toilette' as the French Impressionists called it, and I do not think there was anything corrupt about it. To me, as I assume it was for the likes of Degas, it was simply a scene of sublime beauty. So that evening as the sun began to set behind the pink peaks in the distance, I watched as, silhouetted against the purple sky, Shanti washed her long black hair. She hung forward in her loose green sarong, singing softly to herself, totally self-absorbed as she rhythmically combed out the glistening wet strands. Time stood still.

The scene gave me the same feeling that I imagine I

must have had when my mother would hum quietly to me as a little child encouraging me to sleep after filling myself with her milk, whilst I lay against her breast contented and united. The feeling was of being wrapped in the safety of the nurturing feminine. It was sublime. I think a lot of men long for this, the oceanic feeling of symbiosis we felt with our mothers, and the presence of beauty can lift us out of time and back to that moment. Most of our lives are spent in a battle for independence as we try to separate ourselves from the umbilical cord of dependence upon Mother, and that is often seen as the warrior path of the male. But how many of us men think we have done it when in fact we are still under the spell of our mother country, our mother church, our alma mater, our mater-ial possessions? It is a complicated paradox that we have to separate ourselves from the dangers of unconsciously seeking the refuge of Mother in all manner of worldly things (what Jung calls the 'mother complex'), whilst we must not cut ourselves off from the healthy ability to nurture and be nurtured (the 'mother archetype'). This is why I felt it no sin to delight in the scene before me: it was primal and it was healthy.

Needless to say, nothing in this world is wholly black or white, nothing is that clear cut. On another level my desires were rising again and I half dreaded and half longed for the close proximity of Shanti that was immanent in our room that night. We ate outside under the stars, so close we could almost hear them, and we all agreed it was the best dal bhat that we had ever tasted. The chill of the Himalayan night began to build and it was not long before we all wanted to turn in, everyone was exhausted from the long day's walking.

Shanti and I said good night to the others as they cosied up into the unaccustomed privacy of their own rooms. I closed our door and we both laid our sleeping bags out on to the wooden bunks. I lit a candle and put it on the shelf between us as we clambered into our bags. Shanti did not seem sleepy at all, and wanted to talk even though we could hardly understand a word the other said. I could feel the desire between us like an electric charge, and tried in vain to keep the conversation light. She kept asking me about my marriage and if it was happy, as if she wanted me to enquire about hers, but I avoided such intimacy by steering the chat to our day's walk, and to where we might reach the following day. We parried like this for a long time, but she tired of my British shyness and asked me straight out, for these were words she apparently knew well, 'Do you love your wife?'

I said, 'Yes, of course I do,' and blowing out the candle avoided asking her if she loved Nuru, fearing that she might say 'No' and then what would I say or do? In the pitch darkness there was absolute silence, and the white noise that was ringing in my ears was almost deafening. I am sure that we were both holding our breath. My body was crying out for hers. Then she said, 'Nick, I love you, I want to make love with you.' Oh God! This was tricky!

Here I was miles up in the Himalayas, half a world away from my wife and children, in the most glorious of settings with one of the most exotic and desirable women I had ever seen offering herself to me in love. I was almost overwhelmed with passion. Who would ever know? Was I mad to pass up such an opportunity? Was it against nature? Was it all a crazy dream?

Over the years sex in our marriage had not always been that good or that imaginative, and this was like one of my most erotic and romantic fantasies from those days coming true. Back then I am sure that I would not have thought twice about slipping into a passionate embrace with Shanti. It was passion that I felt was lacking in my relationship. I had been unfaithful twice early on in the marriage, and both times I selfishly felt it was justified because there was nothing happening sexually between Jessica and me. I did it out of sheer frustration, feeling I deserved the break, and as soon as it was done it was forgotten. They were not affairs, just one night stands.

I am shocked now at how lightly I took it all. Nothing like that passes unnoticed whether conscious or unconscious, on some level the psyche of the other partner knows full well what has happened, and the relationship is never the same again. The trust is shattered or worse, some time in the future, the relationship is shattered as happened in my case though it took another ten years.

In our culture the relationship does not necessarily have to end, and we can deal with it in two ways. Either we tolerate the betrayal, turning a blind eye and keeping the relationship going in a dysfunctional way for the sake of the children or for material reasons; or we open up and do a lot of painful hard work by trying to sort out the problems in the relationship. Either way, there is suffering and the dynamics of the relationship must change. To do nothing or to say nothing is the most dangerous course, for sooner or later something will erupt as a consequence of the original action and it will probably have a more devastating effect, as it comes with all the punch of the unconscious. This is the law of cause and effect, which some would call karma. I think this is partly what happened in my case, and the marriage was lost.

I have come to believe that there is no such thing as casual sex. It may be so for one party, but there is always one who cannot take it quite so casually as the other and there will be pain, or the need to suppress the pain through some other form of distraction, somewhere down the line. I learned something startling from Malidoma Somé, an initiate of the Dagara people of Burkina Faso in West Africa. His native culture respects and lives in close relation to the world of spirit, the ancestors, the psyche, feelings, and of course nature: something our culture barely acknowledges and has almost forgotten. He said it has happened that a husband who had been unfaithful to his wife, albeit in a city many miles away, returned home to his village and made love to her, she got ill and later that same night she died. The elders of the village knew full well what had happened and considered the man a murderer. In the real world you cannot hide.

I said firmly, 'No! Shanti, I'm sorry. I am married, and you are married to my best friend Nuru.' I felt that I would have been betraying both my wife and Nuru, not to mention my new Faith. I felt half crazy, but I felt better for saying no. All went quiet, the passions sunk back into our bodies and, satisfied that I had passed the ultimate test, I must have found sleep.

I had a vivid dream.

Jessica was lying naked in bed beside me on my right, and Karin, my first love, was naked on my left. Karin was edging on madness and I was aware that she could not help being anything other than selfish. She was saying that she had to go to see her father on Sunday to celebrate her birthday (which indeed it was in the outer world, it was December 5th). *Jessica became angry and aggressive, she was very strong and she got on top of me from the right.*

Here I awoke disorientated and confused. There was absolute blackness everywhere, but there was a strong pressure on me just as in the dream, and movement. I raised my arms which were outside my sleeping bag and felt the warmth and softness of naked flesh, the small of a back and rounded buttocks.

'I love you Nick, I want you, I want you!' It was Shanti lying naked on top of me. 'I want you, Nick, I want you!' I was all a muddle of angry wives, mad first loves, birthdays and the sweet smelling hair of a gorgeous Hindu mystery who wanted me; and it was all happening in a darkness as deep as blindness. I felt like Othello, *and my fit comes again.* Her body was writhing gently like a snake in the sun, and I moved my hands across her smooth back and onto her buttocks and with some pressure stilled her. I eased myself out of my sleeping bag, and as gently as I could lifted Shanti back to her bed. I said 'No.' It was final.

I awoke in the light of the morning and looked over towards Shanti who was still sleeping. It felt like I had survived a whirlwind, yet everything seemed so quiet and peaceful I wondered if there had been a storm at all. Had I dreamed the whole thing? Then I felt huge relief as it all flooded back to me, and I knew for certain I had done the right thing. I felt an enormous sense of peace. Ten years previously, maybe only ten days previously, I would have believed that by embracing the fantastic situation and satisfying my desires I would have found the peace my soul longed for, but no doubt now in the light of day I would be feeling guilt, remorse, and shame. How ironic and freeing it was to realise that this deep sense of peace had been brought to me by being true to myself, by daring to go beyond the threshold of sensual pleasure and gratification. I had not betrayed my wife, I had not betrayed my best friend, I had not betrayed my Faith, and I suppose most important of all, I had not betrayed myself. Indeed, Shanti had brought me Peace.

Two nights later I lay in my sleeping bag in another teahouse, and a few feet away Nuru and Shanti were lying happily cosied up together in their double sleeping bag, reunited after several weeks apart, and the air was clear around us.

THE FISHERMAN

The Great Fisherman plays us.
He holds us on his line
Invisible, unseverable.
He releases it, long and loose
Only the occasional tug of the tide
Reminds us of its presence.
Then when the storms come

He tensions the line
Making known His Presence.
He gives us time to recognise
That this pull comes from
The greatest lover.
So as we live
We may draw closer to Him
Reeling ourselves in
On this thread
Hooked through our hearts.

Now I just wanted to enjoy the rest of the trek and to get home in time for Christmas. I had found the thread in my life and I had a new sense of purpose and commitment to my marriage, my family, and my work.

We never made Everest base camp because I got a bad chest infection and the increase in altitude was just making it worse. The highest point we reached before beginning our descent back down towards Lukla and the plane back to Kathmandu, home, and Christmas, was the old monastery of Pangboche. Here I had a dream that should have warned me that, in spite of my new resolve, I was returning to a situation that might not be so resolvable.

I have just got back from my trip, and we are having a party. Jessica has been preparing food all day, but I have not bought the wine as yet and it is getting so late the shops are probably shut. Jessica is very unsympathetic and angry that I don't drink any more. In fact she doesn't like it that I've come home. So I go out on to the street to try to find wine, and there I have to run the gauntlet of the enticements of many material things and have to resist buying red sports car after red sports car. I manage to resist the temptation.

The dream seemed to be warning me that there were many more tests to come, and that my marriage problems were anything but resolved. But it also gave me some hope, in that I resisted temptation in the dream and my recent experience had showed me what rewards that could bring.

SIX

Separation

What at first seems a cup of sorrow,
in the end becomes immortal wine.

Bhagavad Gita

Christmas 1988 was to be our last together. Christmas has this myth of parents and children being together, of warmth and happy families. How different the reality often is, but the loss still fills me with grief. In the new year Jessica and I started to sleep in separate rooms. I could do nothing right in her eyes, and she was becoming very hard and resolute. It was obvious that her heart had moved elsewhere. The children noticed of course, and it breaks my heart to think of the trauma it caused them. I recall Hayley, who was about four years old, dragging us together in the kitchen and asking over and over, 'Daddy kiss Mummy, Mummy kiss Daddy.' All children want is for their parents to be together. In a functional family it is what allows them to grow towards a whole, healthy psyche, a balanced yin and yang, the harmony of masculine and feminine energies and qualities. I remember telling Jessica one morning, 'All this is killing me,' and in a sense that is exactly what has happened. It has caused me to die to my old life and, through lengthy self-examination, to get closer to who I really am. It was a gift, but a tough gift.

The unexamined life is the life unlived.

Plato

In June I was up in the Highlands doing photographs for some adverts for the Scottish Tourist Board. The best light is nearly always at dawn and dusk, and at that time of year they are only about three hours apart, and in the middle of the night. So my assistant and I were working very odd hours. On June 6th I fiddled with a poem as I sat relaxing on a hillside above Loch Awe whilst I waited for the light.

ON A HILL

To grow
One must shed skins.
To know
One must sit alone
High on a hill
Overlooking
One's body

Caressed by the wind
Warmed by the sun
The sound of a stream
Cascading downwards
Into the heart
The scent of sweet green ferns
On each breath.
My world, Thy world
Lovingly
One.

On the morning of June 7th we went back to the hotel for breakfast after our night's work. I went to my room to clean up and listened to the news. Students gunned down in Tiananmen Square; mourners cram the centre of Tehran and snatch the body of the dead Ayatollah from a helicopter and pass it around the crowd; Solidarity win an overwhelming majority in Poland and become the majority opposition party to the communists; the IRA are held responsible for a 400 lb. bomb going off in N. Ireland. The phone rang. It was Jessica, nervous at the other end of the phone. First she told me that Joy our nanny was leaving. Then she told me that she was leaving too; she had found another house and wanted to move there with the children. Chaos and upheaval in the macrocosm, chaos and upheaval in the microcosm. It reminded me of the old Chinese curse, *let them live in interesting times*.

I rushed home as soon as I could. This first house fell through for Jessica, but her mind was set and very soon she had found another. She said she needed the space away from me so she could work things out on her own and begged me to pay the rent for her, which I did. I missed the children terribly, but I must admit that it was a blessed relief to be spared the constant bad atmosphere in the house.

My main link with Jessica over the next few months was through her mother, Joe. She and I seemed to have similar interests. Our paths would often cross in yoga and Buddhist meditation groups. She seemed to understand me well and became a bit of a confidante, and I suppose I always hoped that she would be able to put my case better to Jessica than I could. Blood however is thicker than water, and it never seemed to work out that way, everything just seemed to turn sour. It was wrong of me to expect that kind of support, and an undue pressure to put on Joe. I needed to learn to do my own work on the relationship, or on any relationship come to that. Joe and I met up and talked together on and off over the next couple of years, but a dream I had a week or so after our separation told me the way it really was. The news that week had been that the wreck of the Bismarck had been discovered. It is odd how the fodder of current events in the outside world can provide the symbols for the dream realms.

There is a huge old warship on the ocean, it is the Bismarck, and it is Jessica's ship. I am on board another ship, some way off: I am aware that mine is a peaceful ship. The sea is flat calm. I want to communicate with the big ship, but there is no Morse and communications are virtually impossible. I sail my ship closer and throw a line across to the Bismarck. I cross on the Bosun's chair and send a message to the captain. The captain of the Bismarck is Jessica's mother. Jessica is stashed away safely somewhere in the centre of the ship for her protection, and her mother, the captain, is the spokesperson. She gave me a very important and private message that my own ship did not need to know. (Typically infuriating of the dream world, I could not recall the words of the message, but I did know that I would not be able to get close to Jessica ever again). *Her mother was very friendly, and she sailed her ship much closer to mine to allow me an easier passage back. The Bismarck flashed a signal: 'Only one small line of communication left.' As I departed, I resigned myself to having to sail my ship away, as we released the one small line of communication between our two ships.*

I have found over and over again that the dream world is way ahead of the outer world, and the lines that bound us in the outer world took a lot longer to sever. I think it is because we are bound to the gooey domain of dense matter where things happen very, very slowly. It takes a painfully long time for old habits and anxieties to work their way out of the body. Whereas in the ethereal worlds of the dream, the psyche, and spirit, everything can move faster than fast, because there is no friction, no resistance, and no time as we know it. It is where past, present, and future all converge in the Now.

In July I drove down to Devon to tell my parents what was going on. This whole business has been very tough on my parents who, as innocent parties, have lost intimate contact with three of their grandchildren. Talking to them about real things has always been difficult, but this was to begin a process that, in the long term I am sure, has been healing for the whole family. It was summer, so we decided to walk and talk. As it happened we chose to walk in the two places that had played a leading part in my formative years, and my past began to unravel.

To start with we went to Bude in Cornwall, where I was first sent away to school. My father is a keen 'old boy', and has always remained in contact with his schools. I reacted in the opposite way, and have never returned to my old schools. So this was the first time. I knew that being sent away at the age of seven had been a traumatic experience for me, but I hadn't begun to deal with it. I remember the Cornish motto of the school which was emblazoned beneath the leaping dolphin of St Petroc on to our red blazers and our red caps: *fast yn mesk tonnow*, firm among the waves. I remember the gang that four of us formed in our first few terms at the school, we called ourselves 'The Stoics.' God knows what gave us little boys the wisdom to use such a name, but that was exactly what we had to learn to be: Stoics who lived firm among the waves. I remember what a terrible trauma it was for me to be excluded from the gang after what I see now was an alpha male leadership battle which I lost. It had become my security blanket and without it I plunged down into the gloom of homesickness which was forever bubbling just beneath the surface of boarding school life. I remember how I was taken home for a few weeks to recover and my parents took me to a doctor, (was he a psychiatrist?), and I was given a diagnosis of glandular fever, which seemed to make everybody feel better, except me.

So back I went, firm among the waves. I remember the daily walks above the dramatic cliffs and seas of North Cornwall, we went out in all seasons and all weathers. Glorious summers, and wild, wild winters. I remember the master who was the nicest to us, the most entertaining, the one who gave us sweets on those long walks, the closet gay who secretly abused us. I remember the long double lessons when he would read us a good book like 'Kidnapped', and one day when he was reading I desperately needed a pee so, unable to wait an hour for the period to end, I put my hand up for permission to leave the room, but he refused to let me go. Squirming, I eventually reached bursting point and had to run out to the loo, and I returned full of shame to a class of sniggering boys and an angry yet satisfied master. Forever after I dreaded long lessons and exams, my mind always neurotically preoccupied with the fear that I might have to ingratiate myself and rush out for a pee, which of course is exactly what would happen.

The doors of the school were open and my father and I walked in.

Of course everything was tiny compared to the way I remembered it. We nosed around the classrooms, the assembly hall cum playroom, and the old dining room where we found pictures of ourselves in the cricket and football teams we had represented over the years. It was a little spooky. The familiar though long forgotten smells carried me right back to when I was barely more than four foot tall, and I could hear the echoes of all the old voices in the halls and passageways. Then, as I poked around on my own, I found myself in the tiny boot room where the new boys used to hang up their things. I shivered and went numb, I could feel nothing, it was as if an angel had walked over my grave. I didn't know what was going on, and I felt my legs take me out of that room and away from the school as quickly as they could. We spent the rest of the day on the cliffs, walking the familiar old paths that we had trodden daily as young boys.

A day or two later, my father and I decided to go to Lundy for the day. It was the island on which our family used to spend our summer holidays all through my teenage years, and I had not been back there since I worked there one summer vacation as a student. It was a beautiful day, and we walked around the whole island visiting all our old haunts. It is an incredibly romantic place, and I know my father feels it too. It was there that I met my first love, Karin Davis. That afternoon it was as if Karin was walking there beside me, and all the old memories were rekindled.

I have never really got over Karin. The last time I saw her was when I was twenty-three years old and just about to get married to Jessica. I needed to make absolutely sure it was not her I should be marrying. I had been obsessed by her for ten years, in Jungian terms she had become my externalised anima. Still, in my psyche, she is my perfect woman, and my romantic self tells me I can love no-one else. In my eyes she was perfection, I worshipped her, and in a way I still do. This is always a mistake, no woman can bear to be held in awe as a goddess for very long, how can she possibly sustain such a role?

> *The minute I heard my first love story*
> *I started looking for you, not knowing*
> *how blind that was.*
> *Lovers don't finally meet somewhere.*

They're in each other all along.

Rumi

Translated by John Moyne & Coleman Barks in 'Open Secret'

We can spend our whole lives searching for something or someone 'out there' when in fact it is 'within' all along.

We wrote to each other all through our school years, and in one letter she described herself to me as Chaos, capital C. What wisdom in her knew such archetypal imagery at the age of fifteen? Chaos is the goddess who represents the primeval darkness, the formless and confused mass out of which order was created in the universe. That was Karin's gift to me: she has been the catalyst that has driven me on my journey through the underworld, my lady fair, as Beatrice was to Dante. I expect I have spent many years learning to be man enough for her. However, these are realisations I have only had in more recent years, and more of them later. Back then her presence only made me weak at the knees, and I was no match for her. So I went ahead and married Jessica.

As we walked back down towards the boat my father and I rested on a bench overlooking the landing bay which bore a dedication to a young woman who had died whilst climbing on the island back in 1952. The words were her own and were written from this spot, they summarised the romance of lost youth I felt on this island of memories.

Where summer long we knew the paradise
That only we the young and proud may know.

Wendy Anne Mitchell

And on the landing beach that evening I recognised an old friend sticking up above all the shale that had fallen on to the beach from the road-building that had been done on the cliff above in recent years. It was the rock where we all used to sunbathe, and I could see a teenaged Karin lying there, wearing her blue bikini.

I badly needed a break. Tim had told me about a Greek island he had been to the previous summer, where he spent a couple of weeks doing yoga and other workshops in a community of like-minded people. He mentioned particularly the yoga teacher Lisehanne Webster, whom he said was very loving and helpful to him. I didn't have a clue what a workshop was, and I was a little scared and scathing of community living, but it instinctively felt like it might be a place that I could relax and receive some support in what I was beginning to go through. I found out that Lisehanne would be there during the next session which began the following Saturday. So I immediately booked a cheap flight to Athens and found my way out to Atsitsa on the island of Skyros in the Sporades.

On the boat out to the island I met several people who were on their way there too. We began to share a little of our stories with one another, and I started to feel an unfamiliar sense of relief after speaking out some of my angst. With the sun blazing overhead, we arrived at a beautiful group of whitewashed buildings perched right on the edge of the Aegean. There were about eighty of us which was a little terrifying, and those of us who had met on the boat clung to each other for security. In the evening after supper a very casual looking man called Malcolm Stern got the massive group together and made us do all kinds of embarrassing and exposing things to break the ice. Malcolm has since become one of my best friends, but I hated him that night.

Slowly the ice did begin to break, and I spent the first week experiencing the chakras with Lisehanne. This form of yoga was not so much about putting the body into difficult contortions, as about exploring the inner world of the psyche. She calls it Integral Yoga based on the teachings of Satchitananda, and it is a form of therapy. Again, by answering the call of my intuition, I had walked into something unexpected, and it was exactly right for me.

I cried in public for the first time as an adult. I was in a visualisation which took us deep into the heart chakra. Lost in my own journey, I walked through a blue mist and met an angel. It was Karin. Then my little daughter Hayley came up to me and took me by the hand. She led me forward through a tunnel and out on to a high green hill where the three of us stopped. We were all dressed in white and a warm breeze gently ruffled our robes and our hair. There was a beautiful world beneath us and it was this that Hayley wanted me to see. I felt a wonderful sense of wellbeing as we returned through the tunnel and back into the 'real' world. Then when I started to describe my journey to the rest of the group an awful grief swept over me and I began to weep uncontrollably. I felt a fathomless loss which as yet I could not put it into words, but I felt great relief after the crying had stopped. Some of the group held and comforted me, something that not so long before would have made me cringe with embarrassment, but this felt wonderfully healing.

Forgiveness is an easy concept but a difficult practice. I don't believe there is a quick cure-all way to forgive. For me the only way has been to release all the muck of bitterness, hate, revenge and so forth in different forms of therapeutic practice, and to learn to forgive myself for being a fallible mortal, before being able to truly forgive anyone else. The literal translation of the Greek word *aphesis* that the Bible translates as forgiveness, is 'to let go.' Doesn't this give a far better clue as to what forgiveness is all about? However, this was only my first small step in that direction.

FORGIVENESS

The one who's moving
The one who's growing
The one who's shifting in the mind
Is nothing like the one who's left behind.

The pain of changing
The pain of facing
Whatever wells up in the mind
Is nothing like the one who's left behind.

It's in the laughing
It's in the dancing
The dancing is the harvest of the mind
And nothing like the one who's left behind.

The grace of taking
The grace of giving
The Grace that's given through the mind
Is to learn
To love and help the one who's left behind.

The following week I signed up for Malcolm's workshop on relationships called The Art of Loving. I knew very little in those days about the concepts of projection and transference, and I moved quite innocently into a situation in his workshop which was to help me considerably. There were about twenty of us in the group and, as is usual in this kind of work, there were more women than men. One of the women, a Canadian, reminded me a little of Karin. She had the blond hair and blue-green eyes of my typical anima figure, and I transferred it all on to her.

Jung defines anima as *a personification of the unconscious,* which is to say that she is *the intermediary between a man's conscious personality and the depths of his nature, the collective unconscious.* The root of the Latin word for priest, *pontifex,* means 'to make bridges' and is perhaps indicative of the sacred role that anima, as the bridge to the unconscious, plays in a man's life. The Jungian Robert A. Johnson says she might be personified as *whatever name is etched into a man's heart as the one who awakened his soul in mid-adolescence.* Or, in more literal terms, Jung says, *the anima is presumably a psychic representation of the minority of female genes in a man's body.* Anima literally means soul or life, which perhaps hints at the crucial importance it carries for a man's survival.

One day Malcolm suggested we do an exercise which he said might take us back to an earlier moment in our lives. First of all he got us to pick partners through a method of chance, and serendipity had it that I ended up with Joanne, the Canadian. I learned later that I reminded her absolutely of her first love, her animus (the equivalent masculine archetype in a woman), and was therefore playing out something for her too. The gods are always this economical when they become involved in this work, I have found such things happening time and time again. I was to be the first victim. The exercise was very simple, though we prepared ourselves very well for it, setting our intent through meditation and mantra. By that I mean we prayed hard as a group that we would be given the help to do what we needed to do so as to find what we needed to find. You have to be very cautious when doing this kind of deep, potentially traumatic, personal work, and I have learned how important it is to ask for good guidance and protection.

Whatever sets the spirit free
without giving us mastery over ourselves is harmful.

Goethe

We began the exercise. I closed my eyes and gave myself over to Joanne's guidance. Soon I found myself travelling back in time, not like a film running backwards, but jumping back from event to event like a series of staccato still images. I just observed them and they moved on, back into the past. Masses of time seemed to pass, I was outside of Chronos time, but at that stage another part of me was well aware of the pace of things in the room, and we had probably been going only a few minutes.

Then I suddenly plunged down deeper, and I was taken back to my time with Karin and I literally saw her lying on the rock I had only revisited a week or two previously. I felt exactly what I had felt at the time, but this time I expressed it all instead of pushing the feelings down. I felt a bellyaching longing for her, and I cried out to her. I could hear myself shouting for her, totally uninhibited. It was a weird experience, but it didn't stop there. The images started to roll again and I went back through what I can only recall was a mass of darkness. Then, like a whale exploding from the depths of the ocean, a new image breached the surface of my unconscious. I was back to my first day at prep school, when my parents had left me and I was completely alone staring at the wall of that little boot room. I was shocked, I was terrified. My mother had left me there and I didn't know why, nobody had explained anything to me.

'Help! Help! I want my mummy! Where's my mummy?'

I screamed, I kicked and I bawled. Long drawn out screams, suppressed inside me for thirty odd years.

I expressed all the feelings denied to me, all the stuff a little boy of seven was too scared and numbed to be able to do back then. I had regressed completely into it, and when I returned to my senses in a heap in the corner of the workspace I was being held tenderly by Joanne. She stroked my hair, a mother, or I might say a lover, who seemed to have understood completely what I had been through. I was told that I had been in it for almost an hour. I thanked her and, disentangling myself, stood up half expecting to fall back over again, but I felt as light as a feather, as if a huge weight had been removed from my shoulders. I went out into the bright Greek sunshine, stretched, walked down the few metres to the rocks, and dived into the cool Aegean ocean. I stayed under the water as long as I could, and when I surfaced it felt like I had entered a new world. I felt released and empowered, like an eagle.

CROWN TO CROWN

I am an eagle standing aloof
Observing the land below
From the roof of the world
Warm winds stroking my feathers
I am as firm as rock.

I can detach myself and soar aloft
Turning on God given thermals
That are soft and loving
They suspend me in my dream
I can forget my form.

I can lay down by the sea alone
And gaze up at galaxies
Which breathe the sighs of angels
Then perhaps an angel comes
And crown to crown we conjure
Shooting stars.

So that was what a workshop was! I had found a safe place, and my spirit had been set free. I began to dance, and the poetry came pouring out, and best of all I took down the guitar and began to sing again. Many more workshops followed over the next few years as my past continued to unravel.

On my return from Greece I had a dream which showed an important psychological syndrome about which I only became aware some time later.

I was at the top of a tower, back at school, evensong was at eleven, in one minute's time, and I was late. I descended the stairs of the tower and found a door at the bottom that led into a quadrangle. Then, from the cloisters of the school ahead, I heard the echoing of a boy's weeping. It was my son Oliver, and he had just been taken to school and left there all alone. He was crying out his confusion and homesickness. My heart went out to him, and I felt so much sorrow and pain for him, so much love.

Why was Oliver appearing in my dreams experiencing my own traumas? At a workshop a couple of years later I was describing an event that had happened to me when I was nine years old that I had only just remembered. The person next to me asked me what age my son was and I replied that he was nine. Suddenly it dawned on me that I had been hitting all these moments in my life as and when my son hit the same age, i.e. he was seven years old when, in Greece, I relived the trauma I had suppressed at prep school at the age of seven. This phenomenon is not uncommon, and I was very thankful to be made aware of it, so that I didn't project all of my own pain on to my son.

I truly believe that this process of realisation and separating out of our psyches is what can stop the chain of the sins of the father being visited upon his children. My son's presence in my life offered me the gift of being able to see and relive the suppressed events of my own life. However, they were my experiences not his, and it was crucial that I did not pass on my own distorted qualities to him. In my inner life, Oliver was representing my own inner child whom I had to learn to nourish, comfort, and love in the way little Nick had not been by his mother, but in my outer life I had to remind myself that he was Oliver Price who was feeling different things to myself, leading his own separate life, on his own separate journey.

The education of the parents is really the education of the child; children tend to live what is unlived in the parents, so it is vital that parents should be aware of their inferior, their dark side, and should press on getting to know themselves.

To the extent to which they emancipate their shadow, they set their children free to be themselves.

Laurens van der Post. 'A Walk with a White Bushman'

One thing I have learned is to be physical with my children; to hug, and to kiss them. Boys born into my culture and of my generation have often been starved of parental touch from a young age, especially from their fathers. I remember my father touching me once in my life (apart from the formal man to man handshake of course). I was about nineteen and it was after a friend of mine had been killed whilst travelling in the East. He felt awkward and I felt awkward and nothing was said, but when I think of it today it still brings a frog to my throat which is a sign of what has been lacking between us. I know now that not touching cements feelings inside which become the repression of an overwhelming desire to touch, and so it becomes a neurosis. I don't blame my father at all, he is suffering from the sins of his father too, but I determined not to pass those sins on to my children. Boys, men, old men, suffer from a longing to be blessed by their fathers, which need only be a hug, or a kiss on the forehead, or an 'I'm proud of you, son.' How many have received such a blessing? It seems trivial perhaps, but it can be a man's passport to feeling fulfilled and supported in what he chooses to do with his life.

There is an abysmal grief that a lot of men separated from their children have to suffer. It is very hard for men to own up to this and even harder for them to express it. Many men do abandon their families, and for them I have little sympathy. However for most men the epicentre of the pain that surrounds divorce is to be living near to, but not with, their children. Even if they see them every weekend it is never the same as being with them under the same roof in the family home. In fact I have found it almost impossible to rediscover a sense of home without them. So, to avoid this pain consciously or unconsciously, men often feel that they must move as far away as they can, and may even lose contact with their children. These men are not so much abandoning as surviving.

I stayed near enough my children and had them every

other weekend. It was often two days of sheer chaos as they tried to adjust to the emotional change of being with their other parent, and there was usually a lot of shouting and stress. At the end of the weekend, after taking them back to their mother, I would feel an appalling loneliness, an emptiness that I can only compare to the homesickness I felt as a child when I had to go back to school after a day at home. Often over the following years, I would be in floods of tears as I drove back to the cottage on the moors where I was living at the time, and I constantly had to remind myself it was me that was sad, not my children. In a fateful way history was repeating itself, and here was another opportunity for me to relive the pain of the past and to change.

Back in Delhi, the day after I had discovered the Baha'i Faith, still ill and half crazy, I went carpet shopping with Tim. We went to the best shops and wanted to find the best carpets. In the final shop we visited, I rejected carpet after carpet, for I seemed to have an instinct for the good ones, and I was being driven to find something very special. The owner got more and more excited as he rolled out his increasingly expensive rugs. Still I rejected them, until the owner said, 'OK, now I will show you the best silk rug that I have.' He got his assistant to go out to a back room from whence he returned with a rug, rolled up and innocuous looking. He delivered it to his boss who held it up high, paused and steadied himself to make sure he had my full attention, before releasing the roll with a triumphant slap.

I was entranced. An exquisite, fine silk antique from Kashmir depicting the story of Abraham and Isaac in delicious golds and greens. The characters in the drama looked Persian, and all around the borders was a mysterious script that looked Arabic. I wondered what it said and why it had been made, but the man knew nothing of its history. I presumed that it must have been commissioned some decades previously by a Christian or a Moslem to whom the story was familiar. I knew I had to have it, and the seller knew I wanted it. We haggled until I had halved his asking price, then I cracked and he chased me round the room to accomplish the all-important handshake that would seal the deal, for I believe he still thought that an Englishman's word is his bond. The rug is my most prized possession, and for me it has a particular significance that has become more apparent over the years.

It is to do with sacrifice, and in particular the willingness to sacrifice the only son in deference to an unquestioning trust in God. In a sense this has been my journey. Through divorce and all the emotional turmoil, I feel that I have had to give up my son. I have had to live for years with the agonising separation from my son and daughters and, as I revealed earlier, it has acted as a mirror that has reflected the emotional cut-off from my boy-child within. Over and over again, through the deep oceans of pain and occasional thoughts of suicide, I have been asked to trust in the universal process. As I have shed nearly all the things I once had, trust has become the only way left to me.

In the ancient wisdom of the Qabalah or Tree of Life, Abraham represents severity, and Isaac represents mercy, mercy being a stage closer to God. It is an awkward story that often brings up a lot of anger in people. What kind of father would agree to sacrifice his own child? I have no answers to this, but nevertheless the story seems to have woven itself into my life. Spiritual principles and inner truths demand attention, and it is often with great discomfort and self-doubt that I have had to test them, or be tested by them.

The story of Abraham and Isaac is about trust and faith in the creative principle, 'I will be all right, the universe will provide.' The Old Testament fear of God idea is a difficult one to come to terms with in our society, where we see the agony that has been caused by the fear and repression that emanates in particular from some of those representatives who have distorted the ideologies of the various world religions. Abraham's action does indeed seem severe, but is this not mythology? Does it not simply illustrate the lengths to which we have to go to in order to find faith in the Great Provider, or perhaps in Life itself? Here is a chain of patriarchal trust: the innocent, unconscious trust of son (Isaac) toward father (Abraham), and the conscious trust of son (Abraham) toward Father (God). To the conscious human it manifests as severity. Mercy, in the Qabalah, is born out of wisdom, understanding and knowledge, and Isaac's innocent trust of his father seems to be far closer to the kind of trust it would be more beneficial and wise for us to have in the Great Provider.

But the angel of the Lord called out to him from Heaven, 'Abraham! Abraham!'

'Here I am,' he replied.

'Do not lay a hand on the boy,' He said. 'Do not do anything to him. Now I know that you fear God, because you have not withheld from

me your son, your only son.'

Abraham looked up and there in a thicket he saw a ram caught by its horns. He went over and took the ram and sacrificed it as a burnt offering instead of his son. So Abraham called the place THE LORD WILL PROVIDE. And to this day it is said, 'On the mountain of the Lord it will be provided.'

Gen.22 11-14

To suggest that I have been tested in this way may seem a bit grandiose, but I can see no other explanation. One by one things animate and inanimate have fallen away from me: my wife, my children, my home, my business and my old way of seeing myself, until all I really have left is what I stand up in on this particular morning when I get out of my bed, with no real security for tomorrow. I feel crushing fear and enormous doubt, but each day my daily bread is provided. It has been like a snake shedding its skin, and often it has felt too premature, as if the skin underneath has been far too raw to be exposed to the air as yet. Yet I am slowly learning to trust, and to accept the things that I cannot change.

> *God grant me the serenity to accept the things I cannot change;*
> *the courage to change the things I can;*
> *and the wisdom to know the difference.*
>
> *Prayer used by Al-Anon*

Counselling failed to bring Jessica and myself back together and, in late 1989, I set off on pilgrimage to Mount Carmel in Israel to lay my life-changes at the feet of the Baha'i shrines that are built on the side of that mountain. Carmel means 'the garden of the Lord,' and it is there that the Baha'is have created their spiritual and administrative centres. It is the first time in fact that a world religion has managed to have these two facets in the same location. Mount Carmel rises out of the bustling port of Haifa and is crowned by unpleasant looking blocks of hotels and offices, and a busy road snakes up the side of it. However, the bulk of the face of the mountain which overlooks the twinkling Mediterranean now supports many extremely beautiful Baha'i shrines, terraces, and gardens, the Universal House of Justice, the Centre for the Study of Sacred Texts, the International Archives, the Library, and the Teaching Centre. To Baha'is it is known as the Arc of The Covenant and, synchronistically, my time there was blessed with many a full rainbow.

I relate this journey because of a vision I had on the top of Mount Carmel. Whilst I was there I befriended a fellow pilgrim from India who now lives in Canada. She had received shamanic teachings from a native American, and knew many of their ways. It was the day after we had visited the prison cell in Akka in which Baha'u'llah and his family had been incarcerated for many years, and I had been particularly affected by seeing the skylight through which Baha'u'llah's youngest son, Mirza Mihdi, had fallen to his death. To Baha'u'llah his death was a sacrifice.

I have, O my Lord, offered up that which Thou hast given Me, that Thy servants may be quickened, and all that dwell on earth be united.

I was renting an annex room which was situated in the middle of the garden of an old convent on the summit of the mountain, and I had the place completely to myself. When we had parted company that evening, my friend gave me a stone which had a hole in it, and suggested that I meditate with it to see what might happen. She gave me no clues as to the significance of the hole, and these kind of mysteries usually frustrate me, but I thought I might as well give it a go. I lay with it all night in my hand, hoping that I might have a significant dream, but I awoke early in the morning with no memory of any dream at all. However, I decided not to give up, and sat down on the floor to meditate. All this time I had had the stone in my right hand and nothing had happened, so I switched it to my left hand to see if that would make a difference. After all the left side of the body relates to the right cortex of the brain which is said to house the feminine qualities of intuition and feeling.

Almost immediately I was dispatched to a different world.

Everything is blue, aquamarine. I am aware of the sea, and I have a feeling of blissful peace. Soon, however, a gnawing feeling of doubt and anxiety surfaces in me. I am sitting high up on a cliff and beneath me I see a blowhole in the side of the cliff. I look out to the sea beyond, and I can see a huge rock that seems to have erupted from this hole. It reminds me of a blowhole on Lundy called the Devil's Limekiln and the Great Shutter Rock which is supposed to have blown out of it and landed several hundred metres out to sea. I throw a rope down the hole and begin to abseil down, it is at least three hundred feet deep. I see the waves crashing in at the bottom where it is cold and rough. The rope is too short, so I decide to let myself fall the rest of the way on the next outgoing surge. It is frightening, but I know I will be okay. The wave sweeps me out to the safety of the open sea, and I swim towards the large rock. It is as if I have been there before and I am returning. I clamber up the rock, which is the shape of a woman's breast. I climb to the top and rest my head on the soft nipple and my body relaxes. I hear the sea all around me, and feel very comfortable as cool rain washes my naked body.

However, I am still disturbed by a slight sense of anxiety, I still do not feel fully myself. Suddenly I am aware of the presence of a snake. It is coming up the rock towards me, a cobra raising its head as if to strike. It is absolutely wild and goal orientated and I know it wants to sink its poisonous fangs into the breast. As it poises itself for the strike, I know that this is the opportunity for making a change, a transformation. I distract and hypnotise the snake with my left hand, then I grab it below the head with my right. It curls in rage around my arm and body, but it is powerless. I have overcome it.

As soon as I realise this, the snake transforms. It becomes a young prince in white robes, it is Mirza Mihdi. He is vital, noble and wise. He is to be my father. He lifts me easily into his arms, for I am now very small, and he carries me back down to the sea. The ocean is now calm and safe, and we swim back into the bottom of the cave. There we sit cross-legged facing each other, and it feels like he is giving me wisdom. It is pleasantly warm and a golden light is filtering down from high above. He touches my third eye with his finger and gives himself to me. Then we both rise up together effortlessly to the top of the blowhole where the light is pure white. I am back where I started, but now I feel very complete, very whole. I look back out to sea and the rock is still there. I hug my 'father' for the last time and he begins to shrink and disappear into my heart, to dwell there in me.

As with my first vision, I surfaced from this one in floods of tears. I had been awake throughout, and yet it had felt absolutely real. The symbolism is very clear: the return down the birth canal, the oceanic bliss of pre-existence, the penetrative intrusion of the sperm-like male energy of the snake and the call into existence, and the wonderful connection with Mirza Mihdi as my spiritual father. It seemed that I really had travelled through the hole in that little stone, and it was a wonderful gift from some other plane of existence.

There is a tradition in the Baha'i Faith, that if one stands near the sea at Akka as the sun sets and counts forty waves whilst reciting the Holy Name, all one's sins of the past, present, and the future will be forgiven, and this was far too great an opportunity to miss. So that evening, as the sun was going down, I hurried towards the harbour wall at Akka.

Peter Russell in his book 'The White Hole in Time,' points out that the Greek word for sin in the New Testament is *amartano* which is *a term derived from archery meaning to have missed the mark, to have missed the target*. It implies a far more compassionate view of the idea of sin: our aim is not yet true, or perhaps the target has become obscured by the fog of life's pressures so, not for want of trying, we miss the target.

> *The light of the body is the eye; if then your eye is true,*
> *all your body will be full of light.*
> *But if your eye is bad, all your body will be dark.*
> *Matthew 6. 22-23*

We have all made mistakes in the past and no doubt we

will continue to do so in the future, but this metaphor from archery offers compassion, understanding and forgiveness. Anyway isn't sin as a concept purely relative, the way all matter is to the absolute of the velocity of light?

The good deeds of the righteous are the sins of the Near Ones.
Abdu'l-Baha

The forgiveness in the forty waves tradition suggests a compassionate God also, and helps me to be kinder to myself around the mistakes I have made to others and they have made towards me, and makes it a little easier for me to forgive myself and them.

I sat on a huge boulder at the end of the breakwater and counted the waves as they pounded in beneath me. I recited the Greatest Name in unison with each crashing wave, *Ya Baha'u'l-Abha*. The sun dipped beneath the horizon and a chilly wind blew off the sea as I counted the fortieth wave. I could see it coming and it was much larger than the rest. As it hit the rocks it rose above me in a huge plume of spray, soaking me from head to toe as it fell. It seemed pretty significant.

Joseph Campbell defines three stages on the hero's quest, the journey towards individuation. The first stage is separation: separation from the tribe or known community, separation from the safety of mother's apron strings or the safe life, separation from what he calls the programmic self, which is the persona or the mask we wear for the world. The second stage is initiation: the life experiences and rites of passage that bring us closer to being in our true nature, a time of testing and disorientation that often raises more questions than answers. These days, in the absence of wise elders, we usually have to find our own way through this labyrinth, which can be quite dangerous. The third stage is return: return to the community to share the gained wisdom and to put it into action, to be useful. In our society initiation comes much later than is customary in native cultures, and often it comes from the unconscious in the form of a crisis that arises at mid-life.

My separation was more than the mere bust up of my marriage, it was what was leading me into my initiation. Dante knew this place well.

In the middle of the journey of our life I came to myself within a dark wood where the straight way was lost.
Ah, how hard a thing it is to tell of that wood, savage and harsh and dense, the thought of which renews my fear!
So bitter is it that death is hardly more.
But to give account of the good which I found there I will tell of the other things I noted there.
I cannot rightly tell how I entered there, I was so full of sleep at the moment when I left the true way.

Inferno. Canto 1

SEVEN

Law and marriage

We do not become enlightened by imagining beings of light,
but by making the darkness conscious.

C.G. Jung

I have always been fascinated by the paranormal, and during this period I studied it a little with Arthur Ellison, Emeritus Professor of engineering at City University, London. During his talks he explained the phenomenon of near death experience, and in connection with this he mentioned the work of Dr. Elisabeth Kübler-Ross. I knew nothing about her or her work, but only a few days after I left Arthur I came across her name again in a magazine. It was in an advert for something called a 'Life, Death, and Transition' (LDT) workshop to be held several months hence, and in a location that was only about twenty miles away from my home in Scotland. Without really thinking I rang the number and booked a provisional place, thinking that it would be an opportunity to do further research into the fascinating phenomenon of near death experiences. Life has ingenious ways of getting us to the places we need to be.

By the time I checked into the workshop in May 1990 my life had taken yet another turn for the worse. In February I had allowed Jessica and the children to move back into the house, and I had agreed to move out. The children had been showing worrying signs of neurosis caused by the separation and being taken away from their home. Oliver was very insecure and preoccupied at school, and Saskia was spending a lot of her time at their rented house literally climbing the walls. She was continually doing handstands against the wall in what seemed like an obsession neurosis. Jessica still denied any affair with Robert and I felt that there was still hope for us. So when she asked if I would move out, I did so for the children's wellbeing, and in the hope that Jessica would appreciate the good will on my part. In doing this I knew full well that I was giving up the only legal high ground that I had left should the going get nasty. I made sure that she knew this, and allowed her to move back in on the understanding that she would not abuse the situation.

An Englishman's home is indeed his castle, and it was hell leaving it. It represented everything that I had built up with Jessica over the years, and was very much part of my identity. I moved from this beautiful family manse to a tiny soulless one room, kitchen and bathroom flat with a bed that folded up into the wall. It was a disorientating trauma, and in retrospect I think I went into shock. This seems to be the fate of many men caught up in the horrors of marriage breakdown.

A month later I was at a large swimming complex with the children when I bumped into Robert's wife who was swimming with their children. Up to that point, and this was three years on from when I had first suspected the affair, I had thought that she was blissfully unaware of the whole thing and I had never wanted to talk to her about it for fear of disrupting her marriage with Robert. Actually she was heavily pregnant at the time Jessica left me, and now she had another small child. At first we avoided each other, but our children soon discovered each other and eventually brought the two of us together.

Immediately she said, 'Have you heard?'

'Have I heard what?'

'That Robert left me last Christmas.'

'No.' I had not heard. My heart sank and a dark cloud enveloped me as the impact of my blind foolishness hit home. Jessica, still denying the affair, had asked me to move out of the house in the knowledge that Robert had already left his wife, presumably for her. Like a fool I had given her the benefit of the doubt and had now lost all legal foothold in the situation. In Scottish law, once a man has left the family home he has little ground left to stand on. Had I known the full situation I would not have moved out of the house. Fate was playing some mean tricks, and it was making me bitter and angry. I felt naive, ashamed, and worst of all, disempowered. I had lost the only piece of legal ground that I possessed and I wore the cuckold's horns. There is nothing good at all in being in the helpless victim role, it feels rotten to both the self and others, but that's exactly where I found myself, and it brought out the misogynist in me.

A BITTER TALE

They come and trap you
In their spider's web.
Nature bound
They take your seed and let it grow.
Incubation done
They cast you aside
Purpose served
Surplus to requirements.
Time is
For nurturing new plants.

What need have they now of the plougher
The planter
The pater?

Only with the perspective of several years do I see that perhaps this was the only way to break my mould. It takes two to make a marriage work, and it could have been that had I forced things we might have made it work, but given the circumstances I doubt it somehow. My inability to read the crisis rightly, clearly shows the state of denial I was in. I could probably have stayed in the dysfunctional marriage for years. It took Jessica to make the move, which in turn, through a total upheaval, has given me the opportunity to examine my whole life. The Chinese characters for crisis are *wei chi* meaning danger and opportunity. A crisis arises out of something that is no longer functioning well and is crying out for change. If it is not acknowledged the old system may disintegrate and go into total dysfunction, and thus it is dangerous. However there is always a potential payoff to crisis, and that is that it offers the opportunity to examine the things that are not working, to consciously make a change, and thus to move on.

By May 1990 however, my progress was only in its infancy. I arrived at the LDT workshop full of grief, anger, bitterness, and self-pity. I watched and listened as, one by one, a hundred people told their heart-rending stories. The idea of making a study of the near death experience disappeared into the ether as I witnessed in stunned silence the shocking abuses, losses, and horrors that my fellow participants began to painfully emote. Up to that point in my life I really had no idea of the agony that existed in the world. Consciously, mine was only just beginning and it had brought me into contact with this cross-section of Western society that told a hundred different stories all coalescing in one thing, pain.

It took a woman who was expressing the rage that she felt at men to trigger my own anger. In her fury she accused all men of being betrayers. How dare she call me a betrayer when I had been so ruthlessly betrayed by a woman! My indignation rose like brimstone as one of the facilitators led me into another room where I raged and raged at my wife, until a cascade of tears broke loose and I poured out the grief I felt at the loss of my children and my marriage. Like a lot of men my grief was held, deep down and silent, beneath a tight lid of anger.

I was entranced by the magic that happened at this workshop. What began as a Dantesque Inferno at the start of the week with catharsis after catharsis, had transformed into a very peaceful and sacred healing space by the end of the week. According to Bruce Chatwin, one possible etymology of the word catharsis is that it is from the Greek *katheiro*: to rid the land of monsters. Just so! This seemed like real work, the kind of creative work I should like to be part of myself. I was told that if you continued to work on yourself, to face more of your own 'unfinished business' as Elisabeth called it, you could begin to train as a facilitator yourself. For the next five years this is exactly what I did.

During the workshop Elisabeth said that if you feel lost and the going gets tough in life you can always pray for a miracle, and this was to happen to me sooner than I could have expected. After leaving the workshop on the Friday, I had to go straight to pick up my children from various of their friends' houses scattered around town. Saskia was the last to get picked up, and as soon as she was in the car she began to throw an enormous tantrum. She got louder and louder, and very soon Oliver and Hayley joined in too. My nerves were already on a razor edge from the week's work, and I didn't know how I was going to deal with this. I stopped the car and tried to reason with them. It was as if they were picking up on my vulnerability and their agitation was feeding off it, leaving me wide open. I pleaded with them to be quiet, and I knew that if this went on I would not be able to handle them and might have to take them back to Jessica, which was the last kind of defeat I wanted to admit at that time. So I put my hands in the air and silently begged for a miracle.

I drove on, accelerating fast down the dual carriageway that led out of the city. As my speed increased so did the tantrums in the car. At about seventy miles an hour I slammed on the brakes, overwhelmed by the noise and the chaos. I saw red and, skidding onto the slip way at the side of the road, I broke into uncontrollable tears. The noise in the car stopped instantly. I had never cried or shown my emotions in front of the children, thinking that it was not right to do so. From their point of view it must have seemed that I had heartlessly abandoned them, because I had never talked to them about why I had left. Now in the presence of real emotion, a language far more familiar to children than adults, they were silenced. It was the last thing I would have thought of doing in order to stop their tantrum, and I realised that this was the miracle I had begged for. It was as if some deep wisdom inside of them, especially Saskia, had spotted this opportunity and invited it to happen.

I looked at their distressed little faces and said, 'Right, we're going to go back to the flat, and we're going to talk this all out.' So we talked about the separation for the first time, and we all cried together. What was initially painful became healing because the children needed to hear the truth. It is far more devastating for children to be kept in the darkness of ignorance than in the light of truth, and I have been consistently amazed by what they can share and understand. I put out some crayons and paper and asked them to do a drawing, hoping that their pictures might shed some more light on their state of wellbeing. Hayley, the youngest, did an extraordinary drawing.

She drew a large rounded hill, it was green and in the middle were four blossoming flowers, red, purple, orange, and blue. There was a tree either side of the hill, one attached, one unattached. The sky was blue, and there was a yellow sun with blue rays in the top right hand corner. Standing on top of the hill was the figure of a man, he had a smile on his face and looked happy. I asked Hayley who he was,

'That's you, Daddy, on your way home!'

'Who are the flowers?'

'That's me, Mummy, Saskia, and Oliver.'

It was a great relief for me to see her world, in spite of the obvious detachments and separation, looking relatively healthy. Five minutes later I asked her again who the flowers were and she replied,

'Don't be silly Daddy, they're just flowers!'

The doors of the miracle worlds had closed again for now, but this had shown me that the doors were there and so were the miracles, and when I needed I could always ask for more help.

The training I did over the next few years proved to be my line of survival. Jessica was asking me for a lot of money, money I could no longer afford. She was for ever referring to my earning potential as if I were some sort of cash machine that could just carry on coining it in, unaffected by the situation. I could either give in by letting her have the house and everything else and run away as far as possible, or I could stand and fight my corner. We tried couple counselling and we tried conciliation, but our mutual distrust inevitably caused us to become enmeshed in the law, and the lawyers had been watching this whole scenario, circling us like vultures patiently waiting for the kill.

Divorce feels for most men like a discharge, as if one had been fired from a task taken on the day of the wedding. And the agony of separation from a substitute mother figure, the sense of inadequacy among demands for more money, the lack of warmth or grace in the new apartment or house, the felt rejection and isolation as the community withdraws some of its approval and support, the self-doubt the change evokes --- all these add up to a new sort of loneliness. If the man refuses to be cheered up, and considers all of the discomforts to be cunning expressions of an isolating wound received early in childhood, then the man can use the divorce, like any other serious collapse, as an invitation to go through the door, accept katabasis (the bottom, the pits), immerse himself in the wound, and exit from his old life through it.

Robert Bly. 'Iron John'

Interestingly, I was with Robert Bly and Michael Meade on the day I heard the result of my court case which was after three more years of legal battling. I was able to stand up in front of eighty men and explain what had happened. Against the odds, and against all my expensive legal advise, the judge awarded far less money to my wife than she had asked for, and even less than my lawyer had tried to offer in settlement. It felt like some kind of victory, and many of the men, including Robert and Michael, got up and cheered, but as soon as they did I realised it was no victory at all, the cost of fighting my corner both financially and emotionally had almost crippled me, and I guess my wife too.

I hope that I never have to get involved with the law again, but I need to recount a few memories from that experience. I am sure that there are lawyers with integrity, but mine was not a good experience. I went to a lawyer with a reputation for winning, so I suppose I asked for it. People going through the emotional turmoil of divorce are very vulnerable, and the law is a hard-nailed beast that has little time for emotion unless it can be used to advantage in court. Before he even deigned to peruse my papers I had to put several hundred pounds on his desk, and this should have given me warning of the financial demands that were to follow.

I had switched from my previous lawyer as he was a friend and I felt that I needed a harder nut to contend with Jessica's lawyer who had a reputation for being very tough. I had been with the first lawyer for a year and a half for which he billed me his going rate. My next lawyer put in an interim account for the first six months which was more than double the entire bill from my first lawyer. When I queried this he calmly told me that he usually worked for commercial clients, as if that were a reason to charge more money, and then he said, the words slipping out I imagine before he had really considered them, that he also only dealt in 'good quality divorces.' So mine was obviously a good quality divorce! I could just see that phrase coming up at the firm's board meeting as they decided on their business strategies: 'In future we'll only deal with couples who have got a bit of cash, with good quality divorces!'

One day he took me into his own office and I noticed that behind his door he had a chart for his monthly financial targets, and I couldn't help wondering what he might have to charge his quality divorce clients if he couldn't meet his targets with his commercial work in a given month. I complained to the Law Society, and I also discussed the situation with the firm's senior partner who said it did seem like they had charged me an awful lot of money, but neither did anything to remedy the situation. I would have had to hire yet another lawyer to contest it, and I just couldn't face any more of that. Life had become a total battlefield. Someone I had once loved, and still did somewhere in my heart, was now my enemy, and even my own allies were becoming my enemies. For lawyers, accountants, consultants of all sorts, this was payday.

One final memory. I sat opposite my lawyer one day as we pored over the details of yet another attempt at reaching a settlement out of court, when he said to me, 'Look this is the way it is. You have all the moral high ground, but your wife has all the legal high ground.'

'All I want is justice!' I exclaimed.

There was a stunned silence as if I had said something completely taboo in a lawyer's office. Then he rocked back in his chair, guffawing, 'The Law's not about justice Mr. Price!'

I rest my case.

The hardest thing for me to face during this dark journey, this long dark night of the soul, was when Jessica invited Robert to move into our house. It was my outrage that this could be allowed to happen that caused me to find a new lawyer. It felt like a complete betrayal of the good faith in which I had allowed her back into the house. I was powerless to do anything about it, and it had a pretty devastating effect on my self-esteem. I really wanted to kill, and I might well have done so had it not been for the outlet I was given at the Elisabeth Kübler-Ross trainings.

As I already mentioned, one of the prerequisites of doing the training was that you continue to work on your own unfinished business. I had so much unfinished business, both of the past and the present, that my unconscious had become a kind of geyser with emotions and memories bubbling up from the depths seemingly at random. At one of the training workshops, which normally lasted for three days, I did so much emoting on the first day that I had just about lost my voice. The primal scream had erupted. It had been pure feeling without any real knowledge of what it was all about. So by the second day I felt that there could be no more work to do on myself for now, and I would be clear to get some experience at facilitating other people through their own processes. I went to one of the staff members and said that I was ready to facilitate. His response took me by surprise, 'Have you done any of your own work yet today?' Didn't he know that I'd done all I ever had to do yesterday?

Already the room was in full swing, seething with people externalising their grief, their anger, and their pain. I went and sat near a woman on a mattress who was expressing the anger she felt at the man who had abused her as a child. The work is often raw and basic, with people venting their feelings by smashing up telephone directories with hefty rubber hoses.

This woman was deeply upset, and it seemed like she would be there for a long while yet. I sat there wondering what on earth there could be in me that still hadn't been expressed, and I offered up a prayer asking for guidance as to what it might be.

The air around me was full of foul language and the fragmented paper from the phone books. Then a piece of paper caught my eye as it floated gently in front of me like a butterfly gliding down on a summer breeze. It landed in my lap. It was a picture of a red Porsche from an advert in one of the directories. Robert had a red Porsche and once or twice, in the time when Jessica was still denying their relationship, I had seen the two of them together in it. The sight of a red Porsche always set my heart racing and made me seethe with jealousy and rage. Now I just stared numbly at the picture whilst the room seemed to go silent around me. A huge leviathan was quietly ascending from the depths of my being and was about to breach the surface in a furore of spume and sound.

Miraculously the woman in front of me suddenly stopped her work and left the mattress, and before the facilitator had a chance to breathe, I was kneeling in front of him, hose in hand, with the picture laid down before me. I remember little of what happened next. I was told I was there a long time. I hit and hit and bellowed and screamed until there was nothing of the picture left. I killed. It was the homicidal rage that I was not able to fulfil in the outside world. It was the most fundamental emotion of a man whose territory has been violated by another male. Had I gone with a twelve bore shotgun and done it in the civilised world many people would have understood, but I would still have been put away for manslaughter, and it would obviously have ruined the lives of my children.

RED PORSCHE

I sit, I gaze
I wonder what more work that I must do
In unravelling the mystery that is me.
When, fluttering down upon the air
Of another seeker's pain,
There comes a picture
From a battered phone book
And resting at my feet, a butterfly.
It looks at me
Taunting my rest-assuredness
A switch blade into my numb belly,
A red fucking Porsche.

That bastard is in my house
With my kids and my wife
In my fucking bed
And when I ring some mornings
To speak to my children
He answers the phone
From my old place
In my old marriage bed.

Is that not hard?
Is that not enough

To make any man kill?
I feel like killing
And I am not ashamed.
This is natural
I am a proud and angry, jealous man.

But in this seeing moment
In this safe place
I am free to kill,
To pulverise
The red fucking Porsche
And all that lies therein.

And then I can release the victim
That gestates within
And take another little step
Towards the God who brought me to this place,
Who's gift has been to me
All these red fucking Porsches.

Being able to externalise these emotions, I believe, may well have saved me from internalising them in some form of psychosomatic disorder. It is a better thing to let the dis-ease out than to keep it inside.

To be in a passion you some good may do
But no good if a passion is in you.
William Blake, from 'Auguries of Innocence'

After several years I am now a qualified facilitator of this work. I have been told many times that I am a natural at it, but I know it is the darkness I have been prepared to face in myself that has given me the ability to help others through their pain. In 'Walk with a White Bushman' Laurens van der Post recounts how Carl Jung told him that *no one could take his patient further than he had been himself*, and I'm sure that is the truth. The patient does not need to know your life history as the information is somehow transmitted on another plane, the aura perhaps, and they simply know that they are safe to do the work with you because they can sense that you have been through similar things too.

During the last two years of the legal battles I lived alone out on the moors in a cottage belonging to a friend. I had my children there every other weekend, but most of my time was spent in solitude. Photography was still keeping me fed, but I was living off my old reputation and there were longer and longer gaps between the commissions. I did not have the energy to initiate new work, or to go out and sell myself. My self-esteem in the professional world was shattered, even though I could still come up with the goods. Inside I was a nervous wreck, but I was still able to put on a professional face for my business activities, and pretend that I was the confidant Nick Price that people wanted, Scotland's number one; but playing that game took an incredible toll on me. They say that money is energy, and my overdraft was growing to mammoth proportions, which was perhaps a measure of the extent of the drain on my physical resources.

Some mornings I could hardly get out of bed for the

fear and the pain that I felt, but I would force myself up, I would jog and I would put myself together with meditation, and then, if I had work, I would don a confident smile and ply my trade. Sometimes I would curse my resilience and strength, wishing that I could just let go and collapse into the dark vacuum of the abyss, hoping that someone would come and rescue me; but I feared that total collapse more than anything else, as I thought I would never recover from it mentally or economically.

I think the whole period could be seen as a controlled nervous breakdown, if that is not a contradiction in terms. One day a friend of mine brought over a questionnaire that measured the amount of stress a person was carrying in their life, quantified by points scored for stressful life circumstances. For example: Are you divorcing? Have you lost your home? Have you lost your children? Is your business in trouble? Etc. Many points were scored also if you smoked or drank alcohol, neither of which I did, so all my points were scored by the stressful life circumstances. If you scored around twenty-five you had a normal amount of stress in your life, around forty was above average, and around fifty to sixty was positively dangerous. With no points for smoking or drinking, my tally was seventy-five.

I felt trapped in the stress and the emotional agonies, agonies that I now realise have been repeated over and over again throughout my life. It becomes like an aeroplane that goes into a stall and spirals down out of control. Stress consumes an enormous amount of energy, such that there is barely enough left to pull out of the dive. But somehow I would always have just enough juice left in my tanks to pull out before, as I saw it, hitting the rocks and breaking up completely. And of course, fear of disintegration is itself a stressful condition. Thus the spiral goes on and on and on and round and round and round. Struggling along in this situation, blindly surviving one day after the next, is like serving a prison sentence, never knowing when you'll be released.

3rd July '80

This morning I wakened feeling totally exhausted and drained. Getting up I sat waiting for the door to unlock. I couldn't help but succumb to the negative feelings concerning my parole. By the time the door was opened and I was out doing my run I felt physically drained.

I just can't go on. Despair was so deep in me that I sat for a long spell on the rowing machine in a daze, desiring to have a nervous breakdown or something, anything but having to live with how strong I am. I sat there in that condition, dazed, numbed and near to tears but still telling myself that I've got to do those exercises. This is what I hate about myself at times like this; I keep going and live through this torturous situation.

Jimmy Boyle. 'The Pain of Confinement'

Fear of breakdown, says the psychologist Donald Winnicott, is the fear of something that has already happened. Today breakdown is often referred to as breakthrough. When the fears erupt again in our lives, as they so often do in mid-life, we have the opportunity to consciously revisit the original trauma, which is that time when healthy development was interrupted in our life. This trauma if it happened in the first few years of life might have concretised into a neurosis, which forms in us as a defence mechanism to cope with the primitive agony of the original trauma. If we break down in later years, we go back to the feelings that were locked within us back then and, in a pretty literal sense, we relive them. The breakdown itself therefore, is a failure of these defences to hold. These defensive walls have helped us to survive, and any therapy that brings these walls down has to be extremely cautious. A breakdown could be nature's way of doing it; and prevention of breakdown, caused by the fear of breaking down, could merely contribute to upholding and strengthening the state of neurosis. The old saying 'that which does not kill us makes us stronger' may well be true but, like Jimmy Boyle, I was too strong to breakdown completely and that really took its toll.

After two years on the moors I had to move as the friend who had lent me the cottage needed to sell the place. It all happened rather quickly, and I was very lucky to find a little one bedroom flat back in the city near the greyhound stadium in a street that my children and I christened 'dog shit alley' for obvious reasons. Most of my belongings were still out at our house where Jessica, Robert and the children were still living, so I was able to pack all my things into one car-load. As I locked the door and walked down the little path for the last time, the postman drove up and handed me a solitary letter. It had the stamp of my lawyer on it, and I could hardly bear to open it as I thought it was yet another bill. However I sat in my car, and as I said good-bye to the cottage and that period of my life, I opened the letter. It was the final divorce agreement, the decree absolute, all signed and sealed. Life was becoming like Monopoly, 'you have passed go, advance six spaces.' What I really longed for though, was a 'get out of jail free' card.

Elisabeth Kübler-Ross suggests that there are five stages in the process of an individual dealing with a transitional life circumstance: denial, anger, bargaining, depression, and acceptance. In my case this was very much the pattern. The first year or so was spent in me thinking that everything would be all right and we would get back together again sooner or later. I seemed oblivious to the reality of the situation: that was denial. As I began to do more and more work on myself, I started to release the anger and the grief that not only my present situation created, but also the traumas of my upbringing: that was anger. My experience with the law seemed very literally to be a period of bargaining, reducing at the end to a feverish horse-trading over how we would split our possessions. In these material battles lay all the energy of my emotions: that was bargaining. I thought that I had gone through a lot of depression throughout the whole period, but it was only after the divorce came through and I had moved back into town, that I plunged right down into the darkness of depression. Shit makes good fertiliser, but it still smells like shit.

This miry Slough is such a place as cannot be mended; it is the descent whither the scum and filth that attends conviction for sin doth continually run, and therefore is it called the Slough of Despond: for still as the sinner is awakened about his lost condition, there ariseth in his soul many fears, and doubts, and discouraging apprehensions, which all of them get together, and settle in this place; and this is the reason of the badness of this ground.

John Bunyan. 'A Pilgrim's Progress'

Just when I expected a sense of relief because all the battling was over, I became petrified, literally frozen stone hard by fear. The reality of all that I had lost struck me at a deep level. It felt as if I was on the verge of insanity. I can only assume that the settlement of the divorce softened my defences, allowing through some of my most buried feelings: that was depression. And acceptance? Well, that was still some way off.

In mediaeval times the state of melancholia was a legitimate state of mind. It was believed that it could bring you closer to the Divine. Depression in our culture has become unacceptable to most, we are considered ill if we are not up and bouncing the whole time. I dare say there is a place for drugs and electroconvulsive therapy in the treatment of chronic depression, and antidepressants do give the body a chance to recover chemically; but what divine influxes do we miss when we Prozac our feelings away? Society becomes polarised either towards the numbness of feeling nothing, or to the escape of euphoric drugs, and this becomes the norm, such that those who choose to face the pain and go through the suffering, the depression, the melancholia, become the feared outcasts of society. If you manage to steer clear of the drugs and the ECT, then it might be best to seek out your own society of like minds with whom to share your journey, so you don't spiral down and become totally isolated and in fear for your sanity. For me support came from a men's group I had joined. We met regularly every ten days or so, accompanying each other through the peaks and troughs of our lives.

It was at this time that I was drawn to reading books

about imprisonment. From the darkness of my own prison cell of depression I became engrossed in Jimmy Boyle's 'A Sense of Freedom' and Brian Keenan's 'An Evil Cradling.' Perhaps sharing in their extreme circumstances helped me to cope with my own seemingly less traumatic situation. The difference seemed to be that they could see their prison walls. Mine were far more difficult to define, and I am not sure that helped because it gave me nothing solid to kick against. The world outside seemed to be saying, 'Pull your socks up man, and snap out of it!' But all my energy was taken up by clawing at the sides of the Abyss to try to save myself from sliding all the way down.

Synchronicity no longer took me by surprise, and when the phone rang and I was asked to take a photograph inside the lifers' block of Edinburgh's Saughton Jail for a crime prevention advertising campaign, I could only hold my hands up to the angels and say, 'Okay! Why not?' So, in the midst of all this reading and this state of mind, I was given the opportunity to see inside a prison at first hand.

On the way to the lifers' block we walked through a couple of the short-term halls. The men there seemed completely unsettled. The deafening noise and the frenetic activity was pandemonium, it felt a little like the chaos of denial, anger, and bargaining all rolled into one. With the jangling of keys and the clanking of security gates we moved on through towards the lifers' hall. It couldn't have been more different. You could hear a pin drop. The peace was strange though, and most of the men we saw there looked at us from what felt like a state of long established icy silence. Their feelings no doubt lay buried beneath depression, and their acceptance was more likely a numb resignation. One huge powerful looking man had been leaning against his cell door, and I watched as he walked slowly down to one of the prison officers by the entrance gate and picked up a postcard which, as he passed me, I noticed only had one word on it. He walked silently back to his original position settling back against his cell door and stared at his one word. I suppose this was the highlight of his day. I felt the static of his contained emotions. God knows what crime he had committed, but here I was feeling compassion for him. The peace of the lifers' block was built on suppression.

After the men had been banged up I did a photograph of the eerie emptiness of their prison hall. It scared me that this was the stark totality of their world, but would this picture make a young offender think twice before committing a crime? I asked to be shown a cell that might act as a more fearsome deterrent, and a guard took me down to solitary. The cell smelled dreadful. If the dying soul has a smell to it, that would be it. There was a piece of thin foam on a narrow bunk, a small chair made out of cardboard, and a plastic bucket in the corner served as the loo. In the centre of the ceiling was a grill with a harsh bare light behind it, which may well have been left on all the time. Standing in the middle of the cell and raising my arms, I could touch all four walls with my fingers. Thick walls and two solid doors separated it from the passageway outside. It was completely soundproof, and a man could scream himself hoarse in there and not be heard. The only way a man could hurt himself physically in that tiny cell would be to bash his head against the wall, as I'm sure many had been driven to do.

I set up an emotive picture of a man looking very despondent on the bunk. It was horribly oppressive. After three hours the acrid smell, the harsh light, and the silence, created an unbearable claustrophobia. We both had bad headaches and were extremely relieved to get finished. I can't imagine how it would be to spend three weeks in there. The fact was though, that fate had enabled me to experience a metaphor for what I had been living through. I had photographed my own isolation and depression, and now I could see it with some perspective.

Synchronicity came to my door again less than a week later when I had the chance to meet the prisoner inside myself. A colleague of mine rang me to say an old friend of hers had escaped from prison and would I like to meet this man before he gave himself up, as was his intention. We spent several hours together. He was a man of gypsy descent, with a well-developed sense of intuition. He had been jailed for murder. Ironically he had been watching me the previous week doing the photographs inside the lifers' block. I was struck by his gentleness and sensitivity, and we talked passionately like old friends. With him I was able to talk about prison walls, he pointed out how he could see his but that I could not see mine. Despite the sense of injustice that had been visited upon him, for he considered it justifiable homicide, he had an optimism about life that astounded me and that I was not able to share with him right then.

Two men looked out from prison bars,
One saw mud, the other saw stars.

Anon

And it surprised me when this man who was attracting 'dangerous killer on the run' headlines, an outlaw in fear of being caught at any moment, showed patient compassion towards my own situation. I hope that I was able to give him some kind of help too, but it seemed that he had been sent as a messenger to me from the darkness of my unconscious, the lifers' block inside myself. We recognised each other as fellow travellers. He had committed a crime of passion, something I had thought twice about and he had not. I realized 'there, but for the grace of God, go I,' and thanked God for the Elisabeth Kübler-Ross workshops.

Were all these events and opportunities mere coincidences? I think the closer we get to the reality of existence the more so-called real life becomes the dream, and the dream becomes real life. The inner world and the outer world begin to fuse into one. I went to see a film called Falling Down. In it a man who calls himself De-fens has separated from his family and, cracking under the strain, goes berserk with a gun. He takes the law into his own hands as he feels he will get no justice through the system. In one scene he watches an old video of happier married days when he gives his daughter a puppy for her birthday. It was almost an exact replay of the time I gave Saskia a puppy for her fourth birthday. I placed the little ball of fur wrapped in paper gently on her knee, and I'll never forget the surprise and delight on her face when the parcel moved and whined. The kind of magic moment of which both De-fens and I now felt robbed. He ended up committing suicide, and again I thought, 'there, but for the grace of God, go I.' I got back from the cinema to find a message on my machine from a friend in Germany. For some reason, quite out of the blue, he had left me this simple message.

When the law is wrong, the thinking person's place is in prison.

Plato

I was in prison, I was in a nervous breakdown and I was painfully conscious of it.

I am dancing on a cliff-edge.
Am I balancing on sanity
Looking down on insanity?
Or is that sanity down there
In the darkness
Gazing up at me?

And I chuckled to myself as I remembered what Rumi had said.

Everyone who is calm and sensible is insane.

EIGHT

Men's work

There is a crack in everything
That's how the light gets in.

Leonard Cohen

The Age of Reason, the Industrial Revolution, and the present day Information Age, have brought to many of us a greatly improved lifestyle. Much of it is the envy of any human being with common sense, and maybe it has all evolved in the only way it could. There is no reason why material development should conflict with spiritual development, but in evolutionary terms it has all happened at an incredible speed, and at a huge cost to our spiritual, intuitional, and emotional selves. Now it is time to redress the balance, our stressed out states of mind are telling us this loud and clear.

After dark, one evening in London, I was travelling in a

taxi through Soho. Absentmindedly I looked out at the streets as I chatted to a friend. I gazed at strip clubs, neon lights, and street life. Then I did a double take as something out of place caught my eye. A tall black man, head held high, was walking elegantly past a group of people queuing outside a cinema. They didn't know where to look, and were desperately trying to ignore him. He was completely naked, his penis standing hugely erect and proud, and he seemed oblivious to all the people around him. He bore himself with an ancient dignity and seemed completely unashamed, as if this was the most natural thing on earth for him to be doing. The glimpse I had must have lasted less than five seconds as my taxi sped past, but I can still see the scene as clearly as I did then. It reminded me of Leni Riefenstahl's images of the Nuba people of Africa, photographs that always fascinated me.

Of course I don't know what the true circumstances of this incident were, but what I saw made me feel very sad. I recognised something of myself in that man, my lost primitive self I suppose. It was the literal black and white contrast of the surreal scene: the blatant unabashed native dignity of the black man, against the civilised reserve of the crowd of clothed white people who were about to enter the blacked-out cinema, no doubt to witness scenes of sensual pleasure from the sanctuary of the darkness. It was a live metaphor for how confused we've become in Western culture, and how disconnected we are from our natural selves.

By 'nature' I don't just mean sexuality as we express it in those kind of cinemas. I believe sexual energy is just one form of expression of the universal energy that pervades the entire cosmos. All and everything resonates to this force. It is called by many different names: life-force, vital force, chi, prana, libido, orgone energy etc. Ironically, by suppressing sexual energy and putting it down into the darkness, we have given it an emphasis and power that has it spewing out from the shadow of our culture in countless disturbing forms of abuse. But this disconnection from our true nature extends far beyond sexuality.

This first man lived in an extraordinary intimacy with nature. There was nowhere that he did not fear he belonged. He had ... none of that dreadful sense of not belonging, of isolation, of meaninglessness which so devastates the heart of modern men. Wherever he went he belonged and, what was more important, wherever he went he felt that he was known. ... The trees knew him; the animals knew him as he knew them; the stars knew him. His sense of relationship was so vivid that he could speak of 'our brother the vulture.' He looked up at the stars and he spoke of 'Grandfather Sirius'... because this was the highest title of honour which he could bestow.

Laurens van der Post.
From Patterns of Renewal
Pendle Hill Pamphlet No.121

For me this was the tragedy of the Masai outside the cinema, he looked so isolated, so out of place, like he didn't belong there. And this served as such a good mirror for the disconnectedness of my own soul. I would have to go down into the darkness and retrieve what fear had caused me to lose touch with down there.

Man has to discover that everything which he beholds in nature, the clammy foreign-feeling world of the oceans depths, the wastes of ice, the reptiles of the swamps, the spiders and scorpions, the deserts of lifeless planets, has its counterpart within himself. He is not, then, at one with himself until he realises that this 'underside' of nature and the feelings of horror which it gives him are also 'I'.

Alan Watts. 'The Wisdom of Insecurity'

Until then I had not really considered my sense of the masculine at all. It had expressed itself unconsciously in the cars I owned, the possessions I had built up around me, and the economic power I wielded as a husband and a father. In the cut and thrust of my business life I could make quick decisions and get things done efficiently and effectively. My desire to win was the classic stuff of the alpha male. This was a kind of blind and ruthless masculinity, and of course I didn't always win, indeed sometimes my heartfelt instinct was to run away and hide from the conflict of business and the prospect of failure. But through the tests in the Himalayas and the traumas of the marriage breakdown, I became more and more aware of the interplay between the masculine and the feminine, and my own need to understand the polarity into which I was born; that is, my masculinity.

I read Robert Bly's book 'Iron John' and became interested in the work of the mythopoetic men's movement that he and others had initiated. I became certain that this work was important not only for the sake of ourselves as men, but for the sake of women too who were wanting men who knew their own masculinity. The feminist movement had been an essential liberation for women, culturally and individually, and women had become empowered by it, but it had left a lot of sympathetic men confused and with a loss of identity. Many men became unsure of the ground they stand on and either defended it too viciously or could not stand their ground at all, and ended up giving it all away. Bly points out,

Geneticists have discovered recently that the genetic difference in DNA between men and women amounts to just over three percent. That isn't much. However the difference exists in every cell of the body.

We know that many contemporary men have become ashamed of their three percent. Some feel shame over the historical past, over oppressive patriarchies, insane wars, rigidities long imposed. Other men who have seen their fathers fail to be true to the masculine and its values don't want to be men. But they are. I think that for this century and this moment it is important to emphasise the three percent difference that makes a person masculine, while not losing sight of the ninety seven percent that men and women share.

Men as individuals are not responsible for all the abuse, wars, and mistakes that have been perpetrated by the patriarchy, and it is not right that they should carry all the guilt and the shame. Like it or not, women have been part of the patriarchy as well, and it is up to both sexes to heal the rift and redress the balance. A gender war is not the answer. Women and men relate at their best when they are residing confidently in their own true natures. As a man I am manifestly biologically different to a woman, so how can I know how it is to be a woman? We are undoubtedly equals, but we are not the same, and it seems daft to try to be the same. I believe that the three percent difference in our genetic make-up is not merely for the purposes of reproduction, but to help us to seek out and achieve unity on many levels. So all I can do is to try as best I can to be myself as a man, in both my masculine and feminine aspects, and hope that the women whom I attract into my life are themselves fulfilled as women.

We are humans living in the heavy, low frequencies of matter, born into the realms of duality. In the Creation Story, Adam and Eve walked in the paradise of The Garden of Eden blissfully ignorant of the painful split that duality would bring forth. They dwelt in the oneness of Being until they tuned into what can be seen as the negative forces of Satan who showed them the attractions of the knowledge of the Tree of Good and Evil, of duality, something of which we can presume only God had previous knowledge. Thus as humankind walked through that new gateway of consciousness it became a being living closer to the image of God; it had the capacity, if not always the capability, to see the mechanism of the whole picture of life.

I liken the 'good' God and the 'evil' Satan to the positive and negative poles of an electrical current. Life is the spark that is induced between the two poles. In order for there to be a spark Satan, the negative force (Satan derives from the Hebrew word for adversary), had to 'fall' out of the oneness of God where positive and negative resided in pre-existent, pre Big Bang, union. So what was once a unity became split into two polarities when it manifested itself in duality, and the life-force was the resonating current that sparked and flowed in between.

I think the unmanifest God contains both positive and negative, and therefore is neither one nor the other but both, and is something, or no-thing, beyond both. After all God is often referred to as the Light, and wasn't Satan originally known as Lucifer, 'the bringer of light'?

From the point of view of God (the unity that gave birth to the duality of dark and light) the universal dimensions in which the spark flies are all still one, but from the point of view of the spark (life as consciousness) it looks very like there are two violently opposing forces at either end: God and Satan, good and evil, heaven and hell, positive and negative, light and dark, hot and cold, sweet and sour, black and white, inner and outer, left and right, up and down, masculine and feminine, you and me, etc., the list seems infinite. Logically, the dark is as much a part of the Whole as is the light, because everything emanated originally from the One.

Mankind appears to have choices, and this is his free will. If he chooses to focus solely on the negative polarity, evil becomes a very tangible reality in our world. In itself darkness is merely the absence of light, but through man evil can become a manifest and highly destructive force. So too with the positive, if man can concentrate his focus upon it, good will become the manifest force. However, if we can appreciate that the negative forces are as much a part of the life-force as the positive, if we can live with the tension and hold these forces consciously in their rightful place instead of denying or suppressing them through fear, surely we can become far cleaner mirrors in which to reflect God's, the Unity's, image.

The wolf will live with the lamb
The leopard will lie down with the goat,
The infant will play near the hole of the cobra,
And the young child put his hand into the viper's nest.
They will neither harm nor destroy on all my holy mountain,
For the earth will be full of the knowledge of the Lord
As the waters cover the sea.

Isaiah 11 6-9

By acknowledging the shadow we can transform it and reintegrate duality. This applies to all the dualities. A man must learn not to fear the female, as he must learn not to fear the dark. He must find and incorporate the feminine within himself, and a woman must do the same with her masculine. Perhaps this is the way to the Tree of Life which stands at the east exit of the Garden of Eden, and to get past the sword that guards it we have to transform ourselves with a sharpened consciousness gained through the struggles we make towards self-knowledge and the balancing of the opposites. If Adam and Eve are to become one again, this time they will be conscious of it.

We shall not cease from exploration
And the end of all our exploring
Will be to arrive where we started
And know the place for the first time .....
A condition of complete simplicity
(Costing no less than everything)
And all shall be well and

All manner of thing shall be well
When the tongues of flame are in-folded
Into the crowned knot of fire
And the fire and the rose are one.

T.S.Eliot

Jungian psychology has revived the archetypes and shown them to be as alive today in the personal and collective unconscious of mankind as they ever were in the mythologies of the ancient civilisations. As we work more and more on ourselves, the defensive armouring and the personae we present to the world, deep-set into the very tissues of our bodies, begin to melt. The dream world is our connection to the collective and the personal unconscious, and any chink in the armour can allow a whole new stream of imagery to gush through. It pays to be attentive to these images, and to seek help in feeling and ferreting out their meaning. I have kept a journal and recorded my dreams since the beginning of this journey in 1986, and have found my dreams to be an indispensable tool in getting to know myself better. I haven't been able to do this in isolation, so I meet weekly with a dream group and as often as I can with a Jungian therapist, and through reflective discussion I unravel some of the messages I am receiving from my unconscious.

Also the men's work has reawakened me to the use of myths, legends, fairy stories, and the great quests of the heroes, in trying to piece together the puzzle of my own life. Today our mythologies tend to show up on the silver screen in movies like the Star Wars Trilogy, but we also seem to be making confusingly dangerous myth out of the instantly available global news gathering systems we now have. Our insatiable appetites for information bring us live pictures of wars happening on the other side of the world. We see the pictures and we hear the sounds, but we do not feel the heat, the cold, or the pain of a bullet tearing through the flesh. Television and newspapers tend to sanitise the insane fury of war, and we are confusing ourselves by perceiving this media mythology as fact. It may have dangerous consequences. Is it coincidence that the firing of Los Angeles in the riots came soon after the 'live movie' of the burning oil fields of the Gulf War in the early nineties? Why have more Vietnam veterans committed suicide since the Vietnam War than died fighting it? Why was it that the Falklands War wounded were not visibly present at the victory parade? It is as insane to think we can hide the realities of war as it is to think we can hide the betrayals in our relationships; sooner or later the consequences will come up and hit us in the face.

If we do not observe history with a mythic eye and bring the conflicts of the unconscious to the surface we can only be in for more trouble. If we can see Adolf Hitler, who was to precipitate such a mythological battle between good and evil, as a terrible archetype that arose out of the shadows of the German psyche, or perhaps more fairly the whole world's psyche, then perhaps we can take some kind of collective responsibility and prevent such a thing happening again. If we do not read myth properly we will continue to put all the bad things 'out there' on to another person, another nation, another race, and not see the trouble that's about to emerge on our own doorstep.

Indeed as I write this, a story is being played out in the courts that may carry such ominous warnings. It is the case of Frederick and Rosemary West, and the horrific murders they carried out in their innocuous little house in Gloucester whilst an innocent world passed by on the streets outside. Please forgive me if this sounds far-fetched but I see an interesting correlation between this case, tribal sacrifice in New Guinea, and ultimately the Eucharist of the Christian church.

In 'The Power of Myth' Joseph Campbell describes the male initiation rites of a tribe of cannibals in New Guinea. The finale of the initiation was to prepare the boys for their first legitimate act of sexual union with a young woman. The girl would be dressed as a goddess and she would lie couched in a specially built hut roofed with extremely heavy beams. Five boys, say, would go in one by one and make love with her, then a sixth would go in and as soon as he was in union with this goddess the elders would take away the pillars supporting the heavy roof, and the couple beneath would be crushed to death. To them this was a sacrifice of the highest sacred order. At the moment of their death, the couple represent a higher state of consciousness, that of sacred union, mystical marriage or *coniunctio* in alchemy, yin/yang in the tao. It has echoes of our own great romantic stories like 'Tristan and Isolde' and 'Romeo and Juliet,' where union through death was a far preferable alternative to love lost and separation in life. After the couple had died the tribe would pull out the entwined bodies, then cook them and eat them! It was a literal and terrible playing out of the tribal desire to incorporate this union of the masculine and the feminine energies.

THE HOLY LONGING

Tell the wise person, or else keep silent,
because the mass man will mock it right away.
I praise what is truly alive,
what longs to be burned to death.

In the calm water of the love-nights,
where you were begotten, where you have begotten,
a strange feeling comes over you
when you see the silent candle burning.

Now you are no longer caught
in the obsession with darkness,
and a desire for higher lovemaking
sweeps you upward.

Distance does not make you falter,
now, arriving in magic, flying,
and finally, insane for the light,
you are the butterfly and you are gone.

And so long as you have not experienced
this: to die and so to grow,
you are only a troubled guest
on the dark earth.

Goethe.   Translated by Robert Bly

Can this *desire for higher love making* not be traced to the Sacraments? Christ sacrificed his body for us so that we could atone with God. Today, in the rite of the Eucharist, we can eat his flesh and drink his blood, so that we might achieve union with God, in a kind of symbolic cannibalism. Christ sacrificed his life; the tribe in New Guinea sacrificed their children; the Wests sacrificed, in the most appallingly warped way, their own daughter and many other women. My point is, just as the most awful aspects of our denied shadow could produce such a man as Adolf Hitler, that if we deny our desires toward sacrifice and union which is so well symbolized in the Mass, if not always interpreted in this way, then such grotesque distortions will forever erupt. I feel that if we do not pay attention to these terrible things that go on in the midst of our society, we do so at our own peril. Judge and sentence the individual offenders of course, but also listen to what they tell us about our own inner worlds.

We have another wonderful myth happening in our front yard at this moment. Since 1981 the world, and the British people in particular, have been living the myth of the fairy tale Prince and Princess. How we all cheered amongst the pageantry and the celebrations back then. Something was stirred deep inside many of us, and perhaps it was that innate desire for the union of the masculine and feminine. There was the mystical marriage materialising in our Kingdom, which was also the kingdom of our psyches. However, over the years the masculine and the feminine have been split apart in our Royal Household, all was not as it seemed. Originally it was Princess Margaret and Lord Snowdon, then more recently it was

Princess Anne and Mark Phillips, then Prince Andrew and The Duchess of Gloucester, and now The Prince and Princess of Wales. Only at the top, in the marriage of the Queen and the Duke of Edinburgh representing the values of a previous generation, does the household seem to be holding together. *Something is rotten in the state of Denmark!* said Shakespeare in Hamlet, a play rife with the tragedy of a disrupted royal household. For better or for worse, the old values are crumbling away like tired sandstone. Keeping up a front is no longer a strong enough container to hold the lava of unexpressed emotions. The media monsters have pitilessly routed out the truth and revelled in the destruction of the very myth they helped to create.

I feel that the Princess wanted too much, and the Prince wanted too little. The Princess of Wales has emerged from her bulimia a stronger and more articulate woman. I wonder how much of her appetite is now satiated by her work with the public? The Prince seems to have a great sense of spirituality and mysticism rooted in a deep feeling for the Earth; but he still seems to cut a rather tragic figure, like a mediaeval knight bound by difficult duties and codes of honour. These codes of honour seem outdated and are being blasted apart by circumstance. It seems that arranged marriages are no longer acceptable to the western psyche. The old order is disintegrating. How healing it might be to the collective psyche if the Prince and the Princess* got together again, but I feel, as in my own marriage, this is not to be the way of things.

* *This was written only a few months before Diana's death, which fired an even greater mythic response in the collective psyche.*

Essentially, we work on three levels: the literal, the psychological, and the mythological. The literal man says, 'My son is an alcoholic.' The psychological man says, 'What part do I play in my son being an alcoholic?' The mythological man says, 'What forms are constellated in the world view that create alcoholism?' Through the last centuries we have moved through the literalism of reductionist science where everything was split into fragments and analysed as separate entities, into the century of psychological exploration and Quantum Physics where all the bits started to come together again and are seen as interrelated parts of the Whole. Now we are moving towards a new mythology where we might see a change into who knows what. If we stay with literalism we get fundamentalist thinking, and look at the dangers of taking Biblical or Koranic writings literally instead of mythologically. The literal is indeed about fact, but there are higher truths to be gained by looking at the facts from a mythological perspective.

Several years ago a rather gullible friend came to me saying that she had heard that peacocks reproduce when the peacock sheds a tear that the peahen then drinks, and by this she becomes pregnant. My friend asked me if I knew this was true. The literalist would laugh her out of court; the psychologist would maybe ask why she was such an incurable romantic; but the mythologist might see beautiful poetry in an image such as this, and in that way derive meaning and a deeper sense of truth from it.

My response came in a poem.

PEACOCK MYTH

The male spreads his fan
and titillates.
The female sees him cry
sips his tear
and mates.

Birds unify
as separates.
He him, her her
they soar
initiates.

The wise one listens
and hesitates.
It is mythology
not fact it
imitates.

For the first half of the nineteen-nineties I was part of a large gathering of men who met each year in the beautiful east Dorsetshire countryside. The first year I sat at the back of the room at the edge of things, tentatively banging a little drum and hardly daring to say a word. Gradually over the years I found my voice, and I made a good friend in a powerful African drum that helped compound the rhythm of the gathering. Finally I worked my way to the front and enjoyed being in the heart of the gathering, and I risked sharing my songs, my poems, and my passions with all the other men, and I dared to offer myself in leadership. I have broken through some of the male taboos concerning homophobia, and found a depth of companionship, intimacy, and love with men that I would never have believed possible.

In the midst of an initiation ritual on a cold October's night, I have emerged with flayed emotions from the depths of the earth, naked, shivering and plastered in wet mud, to be welcomed by the hugs of other naked men around a huge bonfire representing our indigenous village community. Our identities were fused into one, unrecognisable in our skins of caked mud, unified by the rhythm of the drums and the cyclic melody of a haunting African chant. What a joy it has been to hold an ounce of that golden feeling of community that primitive man must have had, and to discover that we have this capacity just below the surface of our everyday lives, lives normally so wrapped up in economic pursuits for survival.

Our capacity to create a significant ritual in a meaningful ritual space does not have to be taught to us but lies already, all ready, in our souls waiting to be called forth. On the periphery I'm Celtic, but peek into the hologram of my genes and trace me much further back and I'm certain I meet together with you all somewhere in the tribal spawning grounds of Africa.

We are the scatterlings of Africa
Each and every one,
We are the scatterlings of Africa
On our journey to the sun.
Johnny Clegg of Zimbabwe band, Juluka

177

We have grown to fear our primitive origins and it has become our shadow. We conquered Africa, we enslaved the black man, and we trampled on his primitive rituals and belief systems. Indeed many of his ways may have been brutal and uncivilized; I have heard it said, for instance, that the Zulus might punish a guilty man by thrusting a wooden steak up his anus until it comes out of his head. It has to be good to progress from such barbarity, but are our own psyches so free of such traits? Indeed it's not so long since 'civilised' man carried out similar atrocities, and evidently some organisations still do. As long as we deny this shadow it will keep arising into our world in inappropriate ways. In Africa we threw the baby out with the bath water. The darkness there scared us so much that we lost all the positive things as well, the body/soul contact with earth, sun, moon and stars. We forgot how to dance and cry, and as the old Celtic saying goes, *never give a sword to a man who cannot cry*. We disappeared into our heads, into the safety of intellect and reason, and the ties that we knotted around our necks cut our heads off from our bodies. In a sense it has become easier for us to have an 'out of the body' experience, than an 'inside the body' experience.

An African shaman told Malidoma Somé that the white man actually went to Africa to heal his psyche, but in his fear and arrogance, instead of finding that treasure, he ended up plundering it instead. He has taken away countless sacred treasures, encasing many in glass vacuums in museums all around the world. Many of these items hold immense power, and goodness knows what is happening to all those energies as they sit in such homogenised settings so far away from home.

Malidoma believes that they will all have to go back to where they belong, and that will constitute part of the global healing process.

The Age of Reason has rid us of a lot of irrational superstition and barbaric injustice, and led us towards all the luxurious treasures of technology. Who knows how possible it would have been to achieve such technological wizardry without the plundering spirit and missionary zeal of the conquering Logos. But with its ambition and aggression, the masculine Logos has run riot in the world over the last centuries, and at what cost to Eros (the life-force), and the Feminine. The Spanish conquistadors gutted South America of its gold, missing all the treasures of the heart. India has been left strangely schizophrenic by the Raj, split between the values of East and West. The Native Americans were virtually annihilated by the wave of white settlers, many of them hungry for gold, their mythologies blown away by the literalism of the conquerors.

One thing we know, which the white man may one day discover,
our God is the same God.
You may think now that you own Him as you wish to own our land:
but you cannot.
He is the God of man, and His compassion is equal for the red man
and the white.
This earth is precious to Him,
and to harm the earth is to heap contempt on its Creator.
The whites too shall pass; perhaps sooner than all other tribes.
Contaminate your bed, and you will one night suffocate in your own waste.

But in your perishing you will shine brightly,
fired by the strength of the God who brought you to this land and for some
special purpose gave you dominion over this land and over the red man.
That destiny is a mystery to us,
for we do not understand when the buffalo are all slaughtered,
the wild horses are tamed,
the secret corners of the forest heavy with the scent of many men,
and the view of the rice hills blotted by talking wires.
Where is the thicket ?   Gone.
Where is the eagle ?   Gone.
The end of living and the beginning of survival.

1854. Chief Seattle to the President of the USA,
who wanted to purchase the Indian territories.

We are now in the Information Age, and for the first time in known history mankind is acting on a global stage. Cultures that have taken centuries to develop have been disrupted or destroyed and thrown into a global melting pot. Psychically we are confused and lost, we do not know who we are any more. Pieces of each other's cultural shrapnel seem to be embedded in each of us, releasing genetic information that has reawakened all kinds of memories that threaten our inherited and acquired worldviews. In this sense the spirit of the colonised peoples is being reincarnated into the children of the colonialists. As Chief Seattle implied in his profound wisdom, is there some divine special purpose in all this disruption?

Look what has happened in Buddhism. In the natural

fortresses of the Himalayas, Mahayana Buddhism matured in refined isolation for over two thousand years. It was as if a fragile aspect of man's collective psyche had been protected, watered, and allowed to develop like a precious flower until its awareness was ready to be heard and integrated on a global scale by the mass man. Ironically, it took the negative forces of a repressive regime in China to extricate this consciousness from its fortress, and within four decades the Buddhist diaspora has spread around the world, touching and awakening the hearts of millions.

Buddhism with its deep experiential knowledge of both the dark and the light, of life and death, has proved to be a sturdy rudder for steering our ship through the rough seas of these chaotic times. With the exception of China, the Dalai Lama must be one of the most unilaterally respected men in the world. (Incidentally he calls the Chinese *my friends, the enemy*, a lovely example of The Golden Rule, to love your enemy as yourself.) Buddhism, in its Zen and Theravada forms as well as Mahayana, has become one of the most acceptable alternative paths, with many of its values filtering into the modern psyche. Who can fault the aspirations of the Noble Eightfold Path: right belief, right intentions, right speech, right actions, right livelihood, right endeavouring, right mindfulness and right concentration? What interests me however, is that it was the seemingly negative forces of the Chinese plunderer that drove this consciousness out of its mountain hideaway. Would it have known when to come out of its own accord without this negative impulse? Or is this the way of the world? It gives me a little hope that, as Chief Seattle suggests, something globally positive may come out of all the warring and plundering of the last five hundred years, and that we might yet make a grown-up marriage between Logos and Eros, reason and desire, masculine and feminine, science and religion.

I once had dinner in a beautifully converted warehouse, the icon of late twentieth century living, surrounded by all the goodies of Western luxury and wealth. Opposite me sat a Buddhist lama, the same age as myself, in his crimson and yellow robes. I asked him what had happened to him in the National Uprising against the Chinese in Tibet in 1959, which was about the time I was being bundled off to prep school. He said they only had about two hours warning that the Chinese were coming for them, so they just dropped everything and ran, heading for the mountains. They spent two years crossing the Himalayas, and he said that his one instinct was to stick as close as he could to his lama, because he had faith that this holy man would certainly survive the ordeal and that might guarantee his own survival. At one point the Chinese were so close that their bullets were throwing up spray all around them as they crossed a river, but by hanging onto the hem of his lama's robes he survived unscathed. He said that if they were lost or wanted to know where the Chinese were, his lama would simply call down the crows, a bird of prophecy in many traditions, and they would tell him which way to go next. Out of the fifteen hundred that left the lamasery in Tibet, only a hundred or so made it across the Himalayas. All that drama was happening for that little eight year old noviciate monk whilst this noviciate was learning about William the Conqueror and the subtleties of cricket.

Another point of interest to me is that as a bodhisattva the Dalai Lama must reincarnate in order to help others toward enlightenment. It is written in the Buddhist writings however that the fourteenth Dalai Lama, which this one is, will be the last. Vicky Mackenzie in her book 'Reincarnation' asked him about this and he replied:

My own rebirth and reincarnation will be definite, but whether or not people will recognise the next Dalai Lama depends on what will happen. Sometimes I feel I might be the last Dalai Lama. If there is a usefulness for a Dalai Lama then naturally people will recognise him. But if there is no usefulness for a Dalai Lama then forget it! Actually I am not that interested in the institution of the Dalai Lama.

It seems that from the standpoint of his belief system he will return, but perhaps into a new modus operandi, and this leads to all kinds of exciting speculation as to what might be coming our way. A new beneficient world order perhaps.

So are the negative forces there to nudge us on through the things we cannot do willingly out of choice? I am not suggesting that evil is absolved because of this. A friend who had been raped told me she had learned so much about herself as a consequence that she was almost glad it had happened, but of course this does not absolve the evil action of the rapist. Jessica said to me soon after she left, 'you'll probably thank me for this one day.' It incensed me at the time but something inside told me that she was probably right. I repeat Carl Jung's maxim, *what we do not do by choice, comes to us as fate.* Could it be that fate may often require the use of negative forces in order to make something happen that we cannot exercise out of our own free will?

It is said that the masculine energies consist of the vertical forces of spirit, symbolised by the phallus. They are clear, quick, sharp, discerning, and penetrative. And it is said that the feminine energies relate to the soul and the body. They are horizontal, slow, sticky, relational, and embracing. The masculine equates with the white and the positive, while the feminine equates with the black and the negative. These are awkward ideas I know, and I write them in fear of upsetting women, but there is no hierarchy implied here. Negative and positive are equals, and it is fair to imagine the vertical and the horizontal forever changing position as they would in a revolving spiral. Each is part of the same whole and neither is exclusive or superior to the other. If you walk towards the light as soul you will cast spirit in your shadow, and if you walk towards the light as spirit you will cast soul as your shadow. Only when you are awakening and holding both the energies of soul and spirit in a single state of beingness are you truly in the light, and when you are in that light and surrounded by it then you cast no shadow. According to the Buddhists that possibility is available right here, right now.

In Western culture it is the white knight masculine spirit energy that has run amok, and it became obsessed by slaying the dragon. The dragon can be equated with the snake in the Garden of Eden, and represents the darkness of our animal or pagan (country person) instincts. The dragon breathes fire, the symbol of passion, so if it dies passion dies too. Would not taming the dragon or making it our friend and ally be a better solution? Then we can retrieve all the other things our fears and denials have pushed down into the darkness, such as the lessons we can learn from the aboriginal cultures that still survive, or the mysteries of the Black Madonna, and their vital energies can be allowed to flow back into us.

Joseph Campbell tells a story from the Rig Veda, the holy writing of the Hindus, where a strange fog appears in the world of the gods. The male gods go to the fog to challenge it with their own powers. The first says 'I am the god of fire,' then out of the fog is thrown a piece of straw and a voice says, 'Burn that then!' The god of fire is stunned when he discovers he cannot burn it. Then another god goes to the fog and says, 'I am the god of wind.' The voice replies, 'Blow that piece of straw away then!' The god of wind thinks this will be easy, but he cannot shift the straw. Then the greatest Vedic god Indra approaches the fog and as he does so it dissolves and in its place appears the beautiful Maya-Shakti-Devi, the Goddess Giver of Life and Mother of Forms. She is the teacher of all the other gods, and reveals to them the force behind the fog which is Brahman, a neuter noun which is neither masculine nor feminine, who is the source of their being and who 'can turn your powers off and on, as It wills.' So the sacred order, the hierarchy, that is proffered here in the Upanishads descends from neuter, to feminine, to masculine. It is God or Brahman that penetrates us all, and relative to It therefore we are all feminine.

Let me give an example of part of my own denied shadow. During my last winter out on the moors, I read James Hillman's book 'We've Had a Hundred Years of

185

Psychotherapy and the World's Getting Worse.' He says many challenging things in this book, but one of the most challenging to me was his suggestion that Joseph Campbell's maxim 'follow your bliss' should be changed to 'follow your fetish.' This really disturbed me. I associated 'fetish' with kinkiness and perversity, and I thought this idea was going too far and even encouraging the abuse of others in order to fulfil one's own desires. Then a series of synchronicities began happening to me.

As if to endorse my discomfort with James Hillman's idea, I watched the movie Blue Velvet that happened to be on TV the evening I read that part of the book. I found it deeply disturbing and difficult to watch. It was about a very sick man who had an obsessive sexual fetish that involved being extremely abusive to women. It left me very angry with James Hillman. How could he suggest that following this kind of path could be the right way to live? I had no work back then, so I had plenty of time to ruminate over his idea and to dive into what it meant to me. The following day I decided to go for a long walk on the moors to try to work things out.

Except for a very brief relationship which I shall describe in the next chapter, after my separation I was celibate by conscious choice for five years. It was a kind of experiment. I didn't masturbate and I got to the stage in my dream world that I could even stop myself having a wet dream. I missed women and I missed making love, but I knew that I was going through so much change and disruption that I was incapable of being in a healthy relationship, I simply didn't have the space in my life. I subscribed to Sam Keen's message in 'Fire In The

Belly', first work out *where am I going?* and only when that's done, think about *who's coming with me?* And I really hadn't a clue where I was going, so it was untenable to have someone with me. In fact the opportunity hardly arose. I was consciously trying to raise the sexual energies by observing them and setting my mind to letting them move up and out into all the cells of my body, and maybe even out into the ether. Looking back, I think I was rather extreme with myself but it was something I needed to experience to this extreme in order to gain a little more understanding of myself. I think we must acknowledge our urges, certainly we must not deny them, but that doesn't mean that we must always automatically and instinctively act upon them. I wrote this poem on the way to Amberley in Gloucestershire in November 1990, so I called the poem Amber Lie because amber is the colour given to the sacral or sex chakra, and it is about my struggle to understand my desires, my Eros.

AMBER LIE

Unburdened in simplicity I sit
And spin the web of my destiny
A soul that must learn repeatedly
To beware the sticky trap of knowledge
And wisdom's endless roads.

Yes I do do battle with my sensuality.
My semen has a greater potency
A power to defy the pull of gravity

A rising sap in this evolving tree.

Yes, women pull me endlessly
Attract me with their eyes and bodily
I long to jump in physically
A simple call restrains me.
It has been shyness
It has been fear
It has been immaturity
Now it is simply purity
An urge for clarity.

Do not pick the fruits before they have ripened, wait
And they will drop at your feet.

It was a freezing February and there was snow on the moors. I drove my car to a gully beneath a rather bleak looking hill, and walked out into the biting wind. Follow your bliss I could understand, but follow your fetish? What did Hillman mean? I realise now that a fetish is not necessarily an object of sexual deviance, its original meaning is more given to a graven image, i.e. an object imbued with a god or certain spirit in native culture. Back then though I felt that Hillman was referring to the former, and this had been compounded by the synchronicity of watching Blue Velvet. It was telling me something, and I muttered away to myself as I strode out across the moors. When I got to the top, freezing sleet blew into my face like tiny darts. I bellowed at the top of my voice to be given some kind understanding, and realised that my sounds were no match for the howling winds.

Then as I turned back towards the road, for some unknown reason I had a sudden memory flash of a man I often used to see near our home in the country. He was a very weird looking man who wore huge bifocals. He used to carry a walking stick that had a sharp tip to it, and he was always foraging around in the base of the hedgerows looking for something, and once I caught him spiking a bit of paper with his stick which he guiltily hid away under his thick coat as soon as he spotted me. It was then that I realised that he was scouring the country roadsides for bits of pornographic magazines thrown out of car windows. This was his fetish, and I felt very sorry for him. It seemed so sad that a man should have to have such a lonely obsession, and I couldn't begin to know how life was for him. I hadn't looked at pornography in years, and that man seemed a world away from my reality.

By this time I had reached the road. I held my hand up against my cheek to shelter myself from the freezing hailstones, and turned my head away from the wind. As I did so I noticed some large bundles of paper that were scattered all over a lay-by on the other side of the road. Intrigued, I went over to see what they were. There, scattered by the winds, were dozens of pornographic magazines. How unbelievable life can be sometimes! I had screamed out for understanding, and within a few minutes a scenario had been drummed up by whatever those forces are that answer our prayers, and I was immediately swept up into an experience that would help me gain a little more understanding.

Almost automatically, like a schoolboy in a sweet

factory, I scooped up as many of the magazines as I could, and hid them under my waxed coat. Then, blasted by the wind and the hail, I made off down the hill towards my car about half a mile away. Now the scene seems quite comical. I dreaded another car coming past, as in those remote parts and in those severe conditions it would almost certainly have offered me a lift, and I had a vision of all the magazines exploding out from my bulging midriff as I tried to get into the car. However I did make it back to my car with my secret bundle, and excitedly drove off back to my cottage where I could pore over the contents by the warmth of my woodburning stove. There he was, the sad little man with bifocals, alive and kicking inside of me.

During the flashback I had of that man I felt completely dissociated from him, but now I had to admit that we shared a similar archetype or urge inside of us. In spite of some of the clarity I had achieved through my celibacy, I was obviously in denial about some of my most fundamental drives. So I think this is what Hillman was driving at: that we must face and own our darkest desires, for in them lies enormous energy, and a clue to what is missing in our lives. Once seen, they can be incorporated in a positive way and become a useful aspect of our being. Least of all we can have a dialogue with these most repressed parts of ourselves and get to know them, before they leap out of us and maybe do damage to another being at some inappropriate time.

I had learned a lot from my experience with Shanti in the Himalayas, and for a short moment I thought I had learned everything but, as seems to be the way of the spiritual quest, I soon realised that it was only one more little layer of discovery. It was only a fragment of the jigsaw that makes me, the man.

NINE

Hex in Greece

All that is visible
must grow beyond itself,
extend into the realm of the invisible,
if it is to find its firm roots
in the cosmic order,
in true consecration.

Richard Wilhelm
Translation from The I-Ching

In sacred geometry there is a motif called The Flower of Life. It is a six-petalled flower. The petals are made up by the convergence of circles, and where the circles overlap a petal shape is formed. When circles of the same radius are repeatedly drawn using the points where they cross each circle, there appears a pattern of six-petalled flowers that continues ad infinitum.

First of all imagine the dot, the point in the centre of a circle. This symbolises the beginning of life, the no-thing, the unknowable, out of which all energy, all matter, is born. So, the polarity is created by the 'Fall' of the negative forces from the One, and the spark that flies between the two forms a line. So now we have a dot with a line underneath it - an i. If we use this line like a piece of string tied to the dot, we can make a circle. This circle can represent the wholeness of the macrocosm, or a single soul in the microcosm (the idea of the Divine Self.) So now we have an i, or i-dentity, enclosed by a circle. The i could be the vertical masculine principle, it is known as the *lingam* in Hindu symbology. The circle could be the womb, the container of all things in the universe, the feminine principle. The masculine can be seen as the electrics, the current between the two poles; and the feminine can be seen as the magnetics, the sticky stuff, like gravity, that binds things together or contains them. When one circle, or soul, meets another circle, they may wish to relate, and so they overlap each other, and this forms a petal shape. This shape is known as the *vesica piscis* where the masculine and the feminine achieve union, it is the *yoni* or vagina in Hindu symbology. So where circles meet we have the continual interrelationship between the masculine and feminine energies, a kind of continuum of sexual vibration.

The Flower of Life seems to be a two dimensional representation of the matrix of energetics that underlies the whole of life. With the vesica piscis it is a motif that appears in many of the ancient systems: Hindu, Tantric, Buddhist,

Tibetan, Moslem and Judeo-Christian. It is perhaps one of the first archetypes that took form out of the Word. 'Archetype' comes from the Greek *arche typon* meaning original pattern. These are not quite the same archetypes as those of myth which derive more from the resonance of human history, but the original forms and matrices that took shape out of the no-thing.

At Abydos some ninety miles from Luxor in Egypt, and now under threat of swamping due to the rising water table caused by the Aswan Dam, there is a temple known as The Temple of Resurrection. It survives beneath another temple built at least six thousand years ago, so it is obviously very much older. Pictured on the walls of the temple is the sexually explicit story of Isis and Osiris. It depicts how Osiris, killed and cut to pieces by his jealous brother Set, is re-membered by his wife Isis. She finds all of his parts except his penis which she has to reconstruct out of clay, then she makes love with him before he resurrects and she gives birth to Horus, the sun-god. It is a myth that describes beautifully the birth of our universe correlating the energies of creation and resurrection (life coming out of death) with the sexual energetics of the life force. On the walls of a very dilapidated part of the temple are images, etched with laser-like accuracy into the solid granite, of The Flower of Life. No one knows how they were made or who made them, but the motif is obviously very, very old.

It is interesting that the grid of the Flower of Life forms a template over which many codes of life can be overlaid. The amino acids, the building blocks of life, all fit on to this template, as do many of the symbols used by the Masons. It has been shown that some of the crop circles that have appeared in recent years can also find a place here. This information can all be found in Greg Braden's book, Waiting for Zero Point. Modern physics has shown that the stuff of the universe can be observed as both form (particles) and vibration (waves), as both matter and energy. So for me, the implication is that the energy vibration of six somehow underlies the energy pattern and form of the universe. This may all seem pretty far-fetched and I am merely speculating, but I find it fascinating that the number six seems to come up time and time again in relation to the life-force, the spark between the polarities.

In Latin the word for six is 'sex.' In Greek the word for six is 'hex.' In the tarot, card number six is The Lovers, which symbolises the union of the masculine and feminine principles. The I-Ching is composed of six-lined hexagrams, there are sixty four of them, each one indicating a different state of change in life. The esoteric number of the planet Venus is six, and of course the Roman goddess of that name was the goddess of fertility, and she became identified with the Greek goddess Aphrodite, the goddess of love. The Svadishthana chakra in Yoga has six petals, it is the chakra sixth away from the primal Om or Word of the crown chakra, it resides in the sacral / genital area of the body. And in Genesis, the who begat whom of the Bible, we are told that God created man in His own image on the sixth day.

The hexagon constitutes a basis for mineral crystals and the carbon bonding patterns that permit organic substances to form. In the ancient wisdom, from whence the etymology of language derives, there seems to be an evident link between sex and the number six. And if the web of the ancient motif of The Flower of Life has any validity, then the implication is that sexual energy vibrates in tune with the very fabric of life. It suggests to me that the sexual instinct is an impulse that vibrates beyond merely the physical, it pervades all aspects of our being: the emotional, the intellectual and the spiritual. To have relegated the sex drive to the realms of evil, symbolised by Christianity's attitude toward the god Pan, has caused terrible disruption in man's psyche; and of course the number six, or six six six has become synonymous with the Devil. Is it not interesting too that Venus, the morning star, is also known as Lucifer? What is this connection between light and dark, love and light, Venus and Satan, and the number six? I got my next glimpse into the meaning of these things in Greece.

Karin had blond hair and blue eyes, and she was a dancer. I last saw her when she was twenty-three years old. In Greece in the early summer of 1990, I had a brief relationship with a blond, blue eyed dancer who was twenty-three years of age. I don't think this was a coincidence. Fate was giving me the opportunity to play out something that was unfinished between Karin and myself. I will call her Hex. Hex was born in July 1967, the year of flower power, and at the height of my teenage infatuation with Karin. I still have a poem I wrote for Karin that same month in 1967, aged sixteen, at school before the summer holidays. It was about my struggle to understand the masculine and feminine back then, and I can remember my English teacher reading it and asking me how I knew so much. Well, as you will see I didn't know that much, but here I was all these years later with a chance of progressing a little further with a woman born at the very time I wrote this poem.

MAN AND WOMAN

The man is interested in the in
The woman is interested in the out
The man sees the effort
The woman sees the result
The man sees the depths
The woman spirals on high
The man grovels in his conscience
The woman exorcises the past
The man is firm set in the ground
The woman wanders wantonly

The man likes only one
The woman must have more

But this is ALL WRONG!
For the man is the out and
The woman is the in

Though this cannot change the plan
Since the man loves the woman and
The woman loves the man.

We stayed together in a beautiful traditional Skyrian

room. It had whitewashed walls covered in china plates and copper trinkets, and the simple wooden furniture was decked with white lace, as were the windows. We slept in a tiny room, cool and dark, behind a decorated wooden screen. Although we slept together and were growing more and more fond of each other, we did not make love. I was adoring the intimacy, it seemed like a long time since I had had such close and loving contact with a woman. Her resemblance to Karin was uncanny, and as a dancer she had taught me how to dance again. I no longer needed the false spirit of alcohol to bring out the dance in me, Hex had liberated it for me such that dance has now become an uninhibited part of my nature. As the days and nights passed by, it became harder and harder to remain celibate, and I began to question the laws and the understanding that I thought I had learned so clearly through my experiences in the Himalayas.

The situation this time was very different. I had been separated from Jessica for more than a year, and she was now open about her affair with Robert. In that respect I felt I was now a free agent. Hex was single and she was a consenting adult, albeit much younger than myself. We had known each other for more than a year, although our friendship had only recently become more serious as she had previously been in relationship with a friend of mine. She was very physical, she wanted me and I longed for her physically, it seemed unnatural and masochistic to deprive ourselves of the pleasure. The energy between us as our circles crossed was electromagnetic indeed.

My hard earned spiritual understanding would not give

way so easily however. It felt as if I might be losing all the precious ground that I had gained. Hex was not attached to any such spiritual discipline, but making love was not something she took lightly either. However, she was keen and therefore the decision was all mine. I still did not have enough faith to obey a law blindly, I had to try to understand it, and for me that meant being as true to myself as I could be. We only had three more days together in this idyllic place, and I prayed hard to Baha'u'llah for guidance, or a sign to help me.

During the day I was participating in an intensive yoga and meditation course with Lisehanne Webster. I would get up and join our group at six o'clock each morning. On this particular morning as I prayed for a sign. Unknown to myself, Lisehanne had been picking up random objects on her way to the group, asking the powers that be that she might find things for each of us that would give us some guidance in our lives. As our meditation drew to a close she told us to keep our eyes shut while she put something into our hands. I felt something soft and light. My inclination was to bring whatever it was up to my nose to smell it. I recognised the smell right away, it was jasmine. Tears welled up in me as I realised this was a direct response to my prayer. Lisehanne knew very little about my Faith, and she certainly knew nothing of the significance of jasmine.

During my visit to the Holy Land the previous year, the one pervading smell was of jasmine. Each morning fresh jasmine petals were sprinkled at the threshold of every shrine and around all the sacred relics, such that for many the scent of jasmine became the sense memory of the Baha'i Faith. This seemed as good an answer to a prayer as I might get, save for hearing a voice from on high speaking directly to me; and there was more. When I eventually opened my eyes, I counted the number of petals on the jasmine stem. There were nine, and nine is the number of Baha. Amongst Baha'is (known as 'the people of Baha') nine is considered to be the number for this age, the number of completion or fruition. In Arabic all numbers have a numerical value: in this instance b2+ a1+ h5+ a1 =9. I felt He was speaking directly to me, and it filled me with awe. I couldn't have wished for a clearer sign, but was He saying yes or no?

Unfortunately I think the Divine doesn't work that way. He/She/It was telling me that It was there to bear witness to my struggle, that's all, and the decision was mine to make. That's the whole point of being human, we make our own choices and from these we learn. It's like the guidance we try to give to our own children. We can offer them the benefits of our own experience and when they are younger we can set down laws and safe boundaries for them, but in the end they must find out about life for themselves and all we can do is be there for them when they need us, and watch as they make their own mistakes and discoveries. What we can offer them is not judgment, but compassion and understanding.

That day we all took a boat trip to some remote beaches around the island, it was a blissfully happy day of swimming, lazing, singing, and chatting. In the early evening our boat chugged up to a small jetty next to a very rustic taverna on a deserted beach. Everybody was starving and we tucked into a luscious meal of simple Greek food. After we had eaten Hex and I decided to go for a walk up towards a tiny white chapel which was perched on a promontory jutting out into the sea. In the chapel we lit candles for guidance in our relationship, and I lit another three, one for each of my children. Then we walked on up to the top of the promontory to watch the sun go down.

On the flat piece of land at the top there was a large round circle made of concrete, its borders defined by small stones. It must have been the place the local people threshed their corn, but for Hex it made a perfect stage. In silence she kissed me on the lips and bade me to sit down at the edge of the circle. She shed her jeans and her shirt and stood at the centre of the circle in her lime green swim suit, her body nut brown in the fading light. Beyond her the ocean broke the golden sun into a million dazzling fragments as it set behind the islands in the far distance. My heart was pounding with anticipation and I knew that she was going to dance for me.

She wove a divine tapestry into the warm air. She began to create another dimension, and we both went to the threshold and slipped through. From time to time she would glide across to kiss me, as if in some way I was earthing and energising her dance. I was lost in time and I don't know how long the dance lasted. At one stage a friend entered the circle, he was someone who had been working with me in the yoga group. He was very troubled at the time and reminded me of an unhappy old Celtic king who was suffering from an unrequited love. For some reason, that felt to me like his own jealousy, he began to throw hard objects at us, especially when Hex would come over to kiss me. Oddly, the objects touched us but were shed off of us without us feeling them at all, as if the dimension we were in did not collude with his world. We didn't even look at him, and soon he gave up and wandered off. Later I wrote this poem about the experience.

THE DANCE

All that is animal
All that is matter
All that is Earth
Danced for me tonight.

She paused alert as a doe
Head raised high on noble neck
Ears pricked
Nostrils sensing
Tasting each question on the wind.
She crept hidden in the savanna grass
The lioness
The Enchantress
The hunter
Sprung for the kill.
She meandered
Stretching tall her neck
Hypnosis eyed, swaying
The cobra
Poised for the strike.
Her rivers flowed to me
She fed me with her kiss

And held aloft her power.
It was my power
That gave the dance its life
But my power
Was nothing in her.
She was alone
Separate, her Self
The Mother, Woman.

Another entered the circle
A welcome guest in the play
A king whom we love
Whose interventions and attacks
Were only on himself.
We were perfect for those moments
Untouchable.

This was Truth, Life.
She drew up the Earth, the Moon
She drew down the setting Sun,
Me,
She made Love.

I was totally enchanted, I adored her, a word meaning 'to worship' that seems to have gold in it. There had been magic in the air and we were caught up in it, a witch had cast a spell, hex also means witch, and now we were both under it. Maybe the archetypes of ancient Greece were close by and we had called something up: Aphrodite the Enchantress, whom

Bly calls the Woman Who Loves Gold, may have been invited into our midst by the spontaneous ritual. I was in love with a golden illusion and it was tricky ground because, right then, I didn't know it.

I have learned since then through experience that Aphrodite, the goddess of Desire, is a powerful archetype. She can present herself in many different forms, and will put a man through many different tests. Ultimately, she wants nothing less than a real man, and her tests are devised to seek that real man out. Ostensibly, she is the perfect feminine form that rises out of the spume of the ocean, out of Chaos, and whose fertility is so strong that wherever she lays her feet flowers and grasses spring from the soil. However, before a man can be with her in that light, I think she shows herself in three basic forms.

It is always difficult and controversial to discuss these issues because it is easy to sound sexist, and to get stuck in the socio-political arena. The only way is to throw political correctness to the winds and to risk the wrath of others. However, it may be best to consider that when I mention a man I am talking about masculine energy, and when I mention a woman I am talking about feminine energy. These energies exist in their various degrees in both men and women, and so the lines are not clear-cut, but generally the traits have to apply to gender and I cannot avoid that controversy. Certainly from my own experiences which I am sharing in this book, the lessons have come in a very classic, gender-specific way.

First Aphrodite appears as a rather innocent and even sad maiden, who is seeking to be brought to life or fired up by the masculine energy. This is like the school dance, where usually it is the girls who wait to be activated by the boys. If the man can do this and the relationship shows signs of progress, she will then use the magic of the feminine to try to enchant him; but there is a trick involved here. If she succeeds in her enchantment and the man buys the illusion then, ironically, he is not the man for her. However, if he keeps a level head, even though she might display fury at his not becoming infatuated, she will know that he is capable of moving on to the next stage of the relationship. For it is a sign that he can see her as a woman, not as an illusion.

Many men find it hard to love without illusion, without romantic projection. It is here that a man comes up against his anima, and must realise that she is an image that only exists inside himself, a bridge that gives him access to his unconscious Self, to his creativity, to the author of his dreams, his authenticity. He cannot marry his anima because she does not really exist outside of himself. It is the anima whom the Enchantress mirrors and plays out, for she innately knows that this can enrapture the man. It is a thrill for the woman to play the anima, because she can hold the man completely in her power, and so she too is in danger of being spirited away by the game. Look at how many Hollywood actresses got caught up in that spell, never able to give up the beautiful image that could so easily capture the hearts of men. In reality though, she can't possibly keep that illusion up forever, and this is why the enchantment has to fail. The man must spot this happening, and must not collude with the Enchantress. Consciously playing with all this stuff is a different matter and great fun, but that can all come later on.

Another way the Enchantress can operate, is to plug into the man's mother complex, i.e. his emotional and physical dependency on his mother. This also can be very seductive, but as Robert A. Johnson points out, *the mother complex is psychological poison to the man.* If the relationship settles on this basis, then the woman will be a caretaker for the rest of her days, and the man will be locked into the dependent child, however big and powerful he might appear in the outside world. When things go wrong he'll want to dive beneath the bed covers to hide from the world, or run back to mama's apron strings for security. This is an enormous temptation and he must have a lot of courage not to succumb to this one. The woman for her part must have a lot of wisdom to see how right he is to say no, because if she is unconsciously carried away in the role of the Enchantress or the mother, this rejection can feel extremely humiliating to her.

Not many people get beyond this point, I certainly haven't for any sustained length of time. However, I do think I have seen the ground rules for the next stage, and they may sound somewhat chauvinistic though I don't consider them so. If Aphrodite sees that she cannot seduce the man with her magic, then she will become totally malleable, and by that I mean soft, responsive and surrendering. The catch here is that she will only respond like this to a man who has progressed this far through her tests. He is a man who must know himself and all the seductions to which he might fall prey from both his inner and outer worlds. Then, as the fairy tales say, he must learn to give the woman 'sovereignty.'

It has taken me a while to understand this concept. In one of the stories of King Arthur and the Holy Grail, a knight, Sir Gawain, rides out to take on the challenge of marrying a witch, Dame Ragnelle. It turns out that the witch is also a beautiful woman part of the time, but as usual when a witch is involved there is a problem. She gives him a seemingly impossible choice. If he wants to have the beautiful woman in the privacy of his bed at night, during the day at court she will appear as the hideous damsel, and he must suffer the jibes of all the other courtiers who will see him as being married to such an ugly old woman. If he wants to show off his beautiful wife to the court and to appear to the world as a man to be envied, then at night she will change and he will have to suffer sleeping with the old hag.

Many of us make one of these choices, because we think there is no other way. How many married couples put on a wonderful front to the world, and live in hell behind the closed doors of their homes. This is what became of my marriage, and this is the choice that is usually made due to our vanity and immense fear of what others think of us. The other option is far more brave, but still very unsatisfactory. It is the path of the loner who, because this is his only choice, claims to not care how he appears to the world as long as he can be in touch with his creative self in the privacy of his own space. He writes, he paints, he sculpts, he writes music that he thinks is beautiful but that the world doesn't really appreciate. Consequently he can become an isolated and embittered man.

The knight is wiser though, and he sees another option. He says simply to the witch, 'You choose.' She is delighted, he has passed her test, and she is released from an old spell and can now become the natural, beautiful woman again full-time. By giving her the choice he has given her the sovereignty, the queenly power of true womanhood. This implies that she is autonomous and independent of his control, that he does not fear her authority, and that he accepts her natural feminine connection to wisdom. He does not do this out of weakness, but out of experience, with understanding and compassion. They are in tune with the ancient knowledge expressed in Buddhism, which sees the feminine as wisdom, and the masculine as compassion. This is something that Western tradition, rooted in the Qabalah, apparently expresses the other way round.

In the Tree of Life of the Qabalah, wisdom is seen to be masculine, and understanding, or compassion, is feminine. In the East, in Hinduism, it is the fiery dance of the goddess Shakti who brings to life the inert and sleeping form of the god Shiva. In Western tradition it is the penetrative male power that is seen to bring to life the unfertilised, inert and melancholy feminine. This symbology doesn't matter that much, as long as we don't take it too literally and start a war. For I believe East and West are talking about the same thing, and it is just that they are observing the creation myth from different standpoints. The East maybe sees things from inside to out, and the West from outside to in. The East looks out through the window, and the West looks in through the window.

At siesta time, the afternoon after her dance, Hex and I abandoned ourselves to love. We were both entranced, and so we went on through the 'entrance' as if it was the only way forward; but something was wrong and when it was over I felt very sad and that I had lost something, and Hex for her own reasons was in tears. In truth neither of us was right for the other, and it would no doubt have been better if we had not made love, for when the relationship ended a couple of months later there was a lot of upset.

We had learned the hard way, and I felt responsible for letting it happen this way. It feels as if I should have known better, but the whole reason it happened, I believe, was that I did not yet know any better, so I will not punish myself over it. I acted authentically, and I learned by my mistake. *Amartano*, I had missed the target. The irony, if not the tragedy, of life is that I had to follow through with my own truth in order to uncover a deeper layer of truth, and it could be said that it was at Hex's expense, even though she took equal responsibility and was as keen to get physically, emotionally, and spiritually intimate as I was myself. Evidently, we both had something to learn.

Everything is innocence.

Friedrich Nietzsche

The laws of the various religions, especially the Golden Rule to treat your neighbour as yourself that is common to them all, are good guidelines to living a simple and uncomplicated life. For those of us who give credence to the holy writings of the world, we have three choices. Firstly, we can have complete faith in our religion, and obey the laws without question. Those who can do this certainly have a simpler life, and leave themselves free to get on and do constructive things in their lives without all the inner turmoil caused by doubt and self-examination. This path often seems easier for people from the Eastern traditions. Secondly, we can obey the laws because we fear the retribution of our God. I feel this is a very neurotic way to live, and is not mature, comfortable, or happy. This path requires giving ourselves over to some outer father or mother authority of whom we are terrified, and we can become blind to our own inner world and end up projecting all things good or evil on to other people, never truly daring to live our own lives. We are stuck in the child mode and, worse still, we will probably try to pass these fears and anxieties on to our own children. Thirdly, we can try to understand the laws through our own investigations into their truth, so as to test out the common sense that lies behind them. This way we may not so much obey them as be them. They no longer come from some outer authority, but are now an integrated part of ourselves, of our own inner authority. As the perennial wisdom says, God is within. This is the path many Westerners choose, and it is an exciting path, but without doubt it harbours suffering.

Use the rules, don't be used by them.

Joseph Campbell

TEN

Damsels, dragons, and the bloodied lance

We're all in a kind of drama perhaps,
in which we're all centre stage.

Dennis Potter. 'Karaoke'

It was three more years before I felt ready to venture into relationship again. It was just after my divorce had come through and I had moved back into town. I had been going through my crazy prison period. All through this time I had been meeting up every six weeks or so with three friends from the Elisabeth Kübler-Ross work. This enabled us to hone our facilitating skills and to continue our unfinished business very intensively. I was with them down in London one weekend when I found myself working on the mother complex. In a sense I was trying to exorcise my dependency on mother, my innate desire to be rescued by the very thing that was actually preventing me from being self-responsible. You can't really exorcise a complex, but you can bring its existence to consciousness which can help you to live with it, thus preventing you from continually projecting it on to other people.

The mother complex resides entirely inside the man himself. This is his repressive capacity which would like to return to dependency on his mother and be a child again. This is a man's wish to fail, his defeatist capacity, his subterranean fascination with death or accident, his demand to be taken care of. This is pure poison to a man's psychology.

Robert A Johnson

This thing had become so much a part of my being that I didn't know myself without it. I think it became thus because I had to cut off so suddenly from my mother when I was sent away to school. It created in me a longing for mother that had to be held silent in my body, and it had frozen like ice inside my being. To this day there is something in me that lies waiting ever hopeful that it will be rescued by mummy. It is a suppressed wail that has a resonance that I think mothering women pick up on, and can still bring them my way.

For years I was unaware of what I was doing. These women would often be around the same age as myself or sometimes a little older. We would become great friends, but later I would find out that they were seeking a full relationship, and that is when the confusion would start. I would be drawing them to me as mothers and friends, whilst they might well have been moving towards me as mothers and lovers; but I had no intention of being physically intimate with them. We would get into a tangle of mixed messages. So, when they got too close to me I would be genuinely shocked and push them away wondering what on earth I had done to make them think that I wanted to be that intimate. Of course this would surprise them and they would be very upset, and usually that would be the end of the friendship. This grieved me because I cherished their friendship, and so I had to do something to help me understand what my part was in this whole dynamic.

On that day in London with my three friends, I became involved in a powerful visualisation in which I saw myself attached to this devouring mother by a very strong rope, like an umbilical cord, and it seemed impossible to sever. I screamed and I ranted and did all kinds of cathartic work in my attempts to get rid of this attachment, but nothing I did was satisfactory and I still felt bound to her. It felt like it was all stuck in my throat. In my desperation I stopped all the activity and quietly went deeper inside myself to speak to one of my inner guides. He is someone whom I imagine as existing in my sacral chakra, he is a tall wise Masai warrior. He told me exactly what to do. He told me that the cord had to be cauterised. He instructed me to build a bonfire in my throat and to let the cord be severed by the fire. Using all my powers of imagination I did this, and the separation felt real and complete. It also felt clean and permanent because of the cauterising.

I was greatly relieved, to such an extent that I quite suddenly felt ready for a relationship again. On impulse, one of my friends and I decided to go to a lecture on abundance that was to be given that evening at St James's Church in Piccadilly. We both felt that we could do with a bit of abundance in our lives, and so it could do no harm to try to find out more about it. It was a pretty full house, and in amongst the audience I spotted Malcolm Stern, who helps to organise these events, whom I hadn't seen for a couple of years. He came and sat beside me during the talk. The talk didn't inspire me that much, but abundance came to me in a different kind of way. After it was over Malcolm said he needed to speak to me about a commitment he had made the previous week.

He had been down in Bath giving a workshop. Whilst he was there he had been staying with a woman friend. At breakfast on his last morning, despairing at the lack of men who are willing to open up and work on themselves, he told me that he was feeling very cynical towards his own sex and had flippantly said to her, 'If I was a woman I'd be gay!'

His friend had laughed and replied, 'It's all very well for you to say that but I'm heterosexual and I'm still in search of a good man, surely you must know some good men who are free and unattached?'

His initial response was 'No, I do not.' But then after some thought he said, 'Well, I do know one man who seems to be making an effort, but the trouble is he lives way up north in Scotland.'

'I want to meet him,' she said.

'Well, okay! I don't see him that often, but the next time I see him I promise I'll give him your name and get him to give you a call.'

So here we were, only a few days later, bumping into each other. He gave me her phone number and made me promise to contact her. He had no need to persuade me, as the synchronicity to what I had just done that afternoon, and the fact that we had met at a talk on abundance, were clear enough signs that I should follow this up.

It was an extraordinary way to meet somebody, like TV's Blind Date. My first contact with Lucy was by phone. Her voice immediately appealed to me as it had the kind of crackle and huskiness that I always love in a woman's voice, to be honest that is how Karin's voice sounded. We then wrote each other letters. She wrote me two pages of seemingly calculated and unrevealing information about herself, but her handwriting was exquisite and I loved its femininity. In contrast I had sent her a scrawled thirty-six page outpouring of the events of the previous three weeks of my life, which included all the prison experiences which had culminated in the cauterising of the devouring mother and the meeting with Malcolm at St James's. I must have seemed like a complete lunatic to her, but somehow a fascination for each other had arisen, and we agreed to meet a month later under the Bathurst Memorial in the beautiful old church in the centre of Cirencester. I love the Bathurst memorial, as it seems to speak of an uncomplicated balance in relationship that existed in a bygone era, and that my patriarchal genes long for.

Earl Bathurst died 1775 aged 91. Served his country 69 years, with honour and ability and diligence; judgment and taste directed his learning. Humanity tempered his wit. Benevolence guided his actions. He died regretted by most, and praised by all.

Alongside, not below or above, is written:

Catherine his consort, by her milder virtue added lustre to his great qualities. Her domestic oeconomy extended his liberality. Her judicious charity his munificence, Her prudent government of her family, his hospitality. She received the reward of her exemplary life.

I can't deny that this kind of balance, the supportive woman behind the man, appeals to me. Is this man and woman in true and natural relationship, or is this simply the patriarchy speaking? And what was I expecting from any potential relationship by suggesting that we meet there?

We were both very nervous, but Lucy said weeks later that I had hidden it well. It was not love at first sight, but I was very attracted to her. For the first time in my life, I felt in control of myself in this situation, it felt more like I was rising in love than falling in love. I liked her voice, I liked her writing, and now I had met her I liked the way she looked, the way she dressed, and the way we talked and laughed together. Animal that I am I sniffed the air, and I liked her smell. It's worth owning up to such basic stuff as this because if the smell of a potential partner isn't right we might as well forget it.

We had both been wounded by life. Lucy had two divorces behind her, from which she had two children. She too had undergone a lot of therapy, and had just completed a training in psychodynamics. It was going to be difficult for either of us to play games with each other. Because of our life experience we were both very cautious, and as our relationship progressed and deepened a kind of dance developed between us whereby when I got close to commitment she would back away, and when she got too close I would back away. Progress was naturally tempered by the huge distance between our homes, but Fate had it that I was able to do a lot of my work in the West Country, as there was a big set-building studio in Bristol that was well suited to the kind of commissions I was being offered back then.

We grew more and more fond of each other, and as we became closer over the months that followed the sexual charge between us obviously increased. A friend pointed out one day, 'There's a real spark between you two!' How true that expression was, indeed the polarities between her feminine and my masculine were causing real sparks to fly, as we were becoming attuned to the matrix of the life-force, the Flower of Life. And it was here that we had to face the ultimate dilemma.

At this early stage of the relationship I was the one who was going towards commitment and Lucy was the one who kept things grounded with her sense of caution. I would have married her there and then if she had said yes. I was determined to stay within the holy law this time and not make love until we were married, and this is where our dilemma arose. Lucy's way was the opposite of mine. She said she could never marry anybody with whom she had not first tested the physical waters. Stalemate! If we both stuck to our guns we were doomed to never marry and never make love. The powers that be are brilliant at setting us up with the most perfect scenarios for the tests we need. So here I was again.

We were two adults in our forties, neither of us wanting any more children, and we were in love and full of desire for each other. We spent a lot of time talking it all through and both had great respect for the other's point of view. We could not help laughing at the cosmic joke. I deliberated for a few more weeks, but the situation was becoming untenable. Eventually, in spite of what I was advised by my Faith, and in spite of my previous experiences, I decided that this was a completely different situation and that I was not being true to myself either physically or rationally. As an adult learning from his own life experience, the Goldmund path, I had to follow my bliss and see where it led. The love we made was beautiful, and nothing like the experience with Hex, and it felt absolutely right. We seemed made for each other.

Of course I will never know now what might have happened in the relationship had I stayed within the holy law. Eventually perhaps Lucy would have yielded to my ways, and we would have married and lived happily ever after. This is one of the agonies of life, that we are never able to see the paths we might have taken had we made another choice. However, I made the choice after careful consideration, and it was made from the heart of my own experience. If things went wrong then this was my truth and the way I had chosen to learn.

The relationship lasted for a year and a half, and the Enchantress had no enduring power here. We got beyond that stage, and neither of us succumbed to staying in those projections. I admit that I would have been very happy to keep the relationship in the enchantment of the first few months, where I was feeling like the empowered male, and Lucy was the soft princess, feminine and happy. Because of the way we had met and grown together it all seemed very real to me. But

Lucy had a dark side and she knew that I had one too, and she was not going to be content until she had let me witness this aspect of her to see whether or not I would turn and run. Robert Bly calls it the witch, and luckily he had given some instruction on how to respond to her.

In the fairy stories it is often through confrontations with the witch or the terrible dragon that young men and women individuate. Usually, a boy or girl who is being tested in such a way has help from the wisdom of some higher power. Cinderella has the help of the fairy godmother against her witchy sisters, Frodo has the help of Gandalf against the dark forces of Mordor in Lord of the Rings. In relationship however, we are nearly always alone together when the rage erupts and the terrifying vitriol of the witch spills forth. Even if we are lucky enough to have a personal mentor, we cannot have them by our side twenty-four hours a day. Bly says the best thing to do when you see this happening is not to engage in the battle, but to say, 'I'm afraid I'm not prepared to stay in the room with you when you're like this, so I'm leaving .... but I will be back.' The last bit is crucial he says, as it is essential that the woman out of whom the witch has emerged knows that she is not being abandoned, and that there will be a chance to talk things through at a later time. After all the witch, as with the dangerous dragon of the mother complex, is as much a part of the man's unconscious as the woman's, maybe he is the cause of it even. So it could be said that she is simply playing it out for him.

My first confrontation with this aspect of Lucy knocked me for six. It was ugly and very unpleasant to be with, it was the antithesis of the soft, feminine woman I was growing used to, and it certainly expressed no desire to be with me any more. This was definitely not the woman I had first met, and yet it was the part that she had been so desperate for me to see. In my previous relationships this kind of fury had been repressed and so I never had to contend with it in such a direct way. It certainly rocked my commitment to her, but I was committed enough not to run away, which much of me wanted to do. So I just took a walk around the block.

It would happen again, but always after these explosions there would be a melting and we would progress deeper into the relationship. I was opening doors I had never before been through with a woman, and it was a revelation that there was always new life beyond each threshold, not annihilation or the empty void. This woman could get extremely angry, and needed to see that I would not abandon her when she showed that side of herself, she needed to see that I would be back.

Many times I did return, but eventually I weakened. As my commitment waned Lucy's waxed and she wanted more from me, and I met once more the woman for whom nothing is ever enough, as I had in Jessica at the end of our marriage. Insecurity and uncertainty found its way in and I was not able to hold the relationship with the confidence I had at the beginning, and as the witch came out more often, exacerbated I feel by my own inability to cope with her, she got the better of me, and the relationship began to go sour.

In fairy tales, as in dreams, each character is an aspect of the self. I have found that life is like this too, so my understanding is that everything that I induced in Lucy was an aspect of myself. Thus the witch was not her, but me.

After eighteen months we went our separate ways. The dragon had emerged from its lair and kept coming back to test me and, sensing my weakness, went in for the kill. I was no longer sure enough of myself to be able to confront it and to chase it back down to the engine room of the unconscious where its energy belongs. So the happy nurturing woman, the princess even, that was truly a part of Lucy, could not feel safe enough to be my partner. Ultimately I was unable to give her sovereignty. In other words, using the language of my own journey, I was still not man enough for Karin.

..... we, however, are not prisoners. No traps or snares are set about us, and there is nothing which should intimidate or worry us ...... We have no reason to mistrust our world, for it is not against us. Has it terrors, they are our terrors; has it abysses, those abysses belong to us; are dangers at hand, we must try to love them. And if only we arrange our life according to that principle which counsels us that we must always hold to the difficult, then that which still seems to us the most alien will become what we most trust and find most faithful. How should we be able to forget those ancient myths that are at the beginning of all peoples, the myths about dragons that at the last moment turn into princesses; perhaps all the dragons of our lives are princesses who are only waiting to see us once beautiful and brave. Perhaps everything terrible is in its deepest being something helpless that wants help from us.

From 'Letters to a Young Poet,' by Rainer Maria Rilke

I couldn't find it in me to help her, or myself, and my princess became my dragon from which I could no longer extricate the princess.

In his book 'He' Robert A. Johnson talks about Parsifal's meeting with the Hideous Damsel and sheds some light on the subject.

The Hideous Damsel is the carrier of doubt and despair, the destroying, spoiling quality that visits any intelligent man at mid-life ...... It is genius in a woman if she can be quiet in the presence of her man when he is going through this dark time. This protects her from the projection of the Hideous Damsel that the man would be only too happy to put upon her .... In our tranquilliser age it is the general opinion that the Hideous Damsel time should be avoided and treated as an illness to be cured. To banish her darkness is to sterilise one's chance at the evolution she brings .... To honour the Hideous Damsel and accept her new view of the nature of the quest is to embark on the second half of life.

According to his view we both had something to learn from our experience together, and our relationship had taken me further than I had travelled in fourteen years of marriage, and had been full of gifts. To honour it, I wrote a poem.

THE GHATS : DYING INTO THE ONE

Sunset
Red light
Smoke and ashes by the fiery waters
Scorpion and Goat, Bull and Lioness
Burned and fused united   slides
On to Holy Ganges.

Full Moon
Moonlight
Phosphorescence on the rippling waters
Sweetly, slowly drifting down to oceans
The body of our love   glides
On the Holy Ganges.

Moonset
Black night
Souls and spirits walking on the waters
Sinking, sinking into silt and darkness
Goes our charcoaled body   dies
Manna to the Ganges.

Dawn break
Gold light
Stillness, silence on the mirrored waters
Sunken substance of our shadow gone now
A blue heron lifts off   flies
Clear of Holy Ganges.

Noon time
Sunlight
Sparkling, dazzling on the dancing waters
Garlands, jasmine, rose-joys of our love-life
Bright, floating memories   sighs
All the Holy Ganges.

There is one more thing I must talk about concerning these relationships, and it too involves the story of Parsifal in the Grail Legends. I have no doubt that on my journey it has been my sexuality, and hence my life-force, that has been wounded. In Parsifal, the Fisher King is wounded in the thigh, scalded by a freshly caught fish he was cooking by a stream. The fish is the symbol of Christ, and the wound here represents a reminder of a spiritual deficit in the King's life. He cannot continue to live his life the way he has been; something, somehow, must change. His wound has drained his energy, and his kingdom has become unproductive, dull, and without purpose. This is what happened to me in mid-life.

I knew nothing of the Grail Legends back then, nor did I know that this was a known path trodden by many men before me. Unfortunately neither did my wife, and she just couldn't see how I could be so discontented when we had achieved so much.

How many times have women said to their men: 'Look at all the things you have; you have the best job you ever had in your life. Our income is better than ever. We have two cars. We have two and sometimes three day weekends. Why aren't you happy?'
The man is too inarticulate to reply, 'Because I am a Fisher King and am wounded and cannot touch any of this happiness.'

Robert A Johnson. 'He'

Even though I read this many years after the event, it has been such a relief to find that I am not so abnormal, and that as far as the quest is concerned I am reassuringly normal, since the path I have travelled seems to have been mapped out over the centuries by many others before me. One of the reasons I am telling my story therefore, is the hope that it might help other men feel less crazy when all these things start knocking at their doors.

In another and possibly earlier version of the myth, the Fisher King was wounded by an arrow that pierced both his testicles. A wound in the genitals indicates a wound to the life-force itself, damage to the matrix of The Flower of Life, it is a wound that de-animates a man. It effects our creativity, our work, and our relatedness to the feminine. To me this indicates the link between sexuality and spirituality, between the earth and the sky. To be wounded in the generative regions is to be wounded spiritually, and to be starved of spirituality is to be wounded sexually, which in fact may mean a lack, or an excess, of sex. The legend continues by describing how the King sits every night in the Grail Castle suffering the pain of his wound, as he watches three fair maidens parade before him.

The first carries the bloodied lance which pierced the side of Christ at the crucifixion. Another carries the dish which holds the bread of the Last Supper. The last carries the luminescent Grail chalice itself from which everyone present drinks the wine and has their innermost wishes fulfilled before they even have had a chance to think about them, all that is except the King. These last two obviously reflect the transformative powers of the Eucharist. The lance could well be a symbol of the phallus, and the blood upon it suggests the wound.

The Grail Legends date from around the twelfth

century, the time of the Crusades, troubadours, fair damsels and chivalrous knights in shining armour. The lance of the knight was his penetrative power, the power to pierce and wound another, his means of impressing and winning his lady fair, and his means of defence. It kept his maleness alive and demonstrated his ability to regenerate himself, resurrection in spiritual terms, and thus it is a truly phallic symbol. The fact that the lance has blood on it in addition to the image of the arrow through the testicles, suggests a terrible wound to the generative potential of the masculine. This all happened very literally to me, and in order to explore the meaning of it I have to reveal something very personal.

Earlier I mentioned the extremes to which I went in my exploration of celibacy, in that I even appeared to be able to control orgasm in my dreams. About a year after my experiences with Hex, and two years before I met Lucy, my sap did eventually break through in my sleep. I had the shock of my life, because it was a dark reddy-brown colour. I went to my doctor, and keeping a brave face but inwardly fearing that I had some terrible disease I said, 'It's so long since I've used this thing that it appears to have gone rusty!' He reassured me that although it might look nasty, it was fairly harmless. I had a condition called hematospermia, meaning that somewhere in the ducts around my prostate I had a burst blood vessel, and blood was leaking into my sperm. If I needed anything to keep me celibate this would do the trick, as I was ashamed at how ghastly it looked.

By this time I was looking at everything in my life symbolically, and this condition hinted strongly that there was a nasty wound in my generative powers. Indeed, because of this, I had to admit that my self-esteem and my sexuality had been very damaged by the rejection of my wife for another man, and now it had become necessary to examine my motives for remaining celibate. I had to be ruthlessly honest with myself, making sure that my path toward spirituality and celibacy was not an avoidance, a word that suggests exactly what it is, a dance in the void, a dance that can bear no fruit. The hematospermia brought me back down to earth. To quench the spiritual thirst is essential, but we have to remain human and stay in touch with the physical world, for spirit involves the whole of our being.

Although I had learned a lot over the years of my separation, and my experiences had raised my spiritual awareness, I had to admit to myself that my life in the world had become pretty barren and unhappy. I no longer much cared about how I looked or about where I lived. In the past I had been obsessed by what colours the walls of my house were painted and what little trinkets were placed on the mantelpiece. Then, long after the separation, I woke up one morning to realise that I had been living in a remote cottage on the moors for almost two years without even noticing the peeling wallpaper and the naked light bulbs. I had been slowly losing all my money and all the material things I had possessed, not to mention a life with my children. Like a short-circuiting electricity supply I was being drained of all my power, and I had lost my place in the world.

Another life was incubating in this seemingly barren womb, but as yet it was unknown and unseen, and like an egg newly fertilised in the uterus, there was little evidence of it. My wound seemed very literally akin to that of the Fisher King, my testicles had been pierced by an arrow, and there was blood on the end of my lance. However, there's another version of the legend that bears a clue that gave me some hope that I was headed in the right direction, for written on the end of the bloodied lance is the word 'Grail.'

I was extremely inhibited by this condition, thinking that it would really repulse any woman with whom I might like to get into close relationship. During the years I suffered from it various doctors prescribed different antibiotics as antidotes, but none of them made the slightest bit of difference. I even went into hospital for a painful examination of my urethra which thankfully gave me the all clear with cancer, but yielded nothing as to how the condition could be cleared. However, a strange thing happened as soon as I made the decision to make love with Lucy. Overnight the bleeding stopped and the condition disappeared. It remained absolutely clear throughout the whole period of our relationship, but as soon as we parted, it returned with a vengeance. I can no longer see such a thing as a coincidence.

I was reading Robert A. Johnson's 'The Fisher King and The Handless Maiden' at the time I discovered the return of these symptoms, and what I read gave me quite a jolt.

Faculty (the new consciousness available to the Fisher King) .... can only too easily slip back into the unconscious and instantly reappear as a symptom, the Fisher King wound, so that the same energy is now experienced as suffering.

I felt this was a dire warning. Initially I thought it was telling me that I was foolish to not go on through the next threshold in relationship with Lucy, that I had learned nothing, that nothing had changed, that I was back to where I was before the relationship had started, and that my wound would cause me yet more suffering.

After a little more meditation on the matter however, I found that it was simply telling me that I couldn't rest on my laurels. It was essential that I stay vigilant and continue to live on every level, from the physical through to the spiritual, in the new consciousness that I had acquired through all of my experiences. And yes, anything forgotten or taken for granted could return back down to the unconscious and cause even worse suffering than it had before it was first uncovered.

Another clue to the meaning of the Fisher King wound comes from a comparable story in Greek myth. It is the story of Chiron. Chiron was an immortal, the king of the Centaurs, half god-man, half horse. The horse part of himself gave him the benefit of clearly knowing the potency of the animal kingdom, and this close relationship with Nature gave him a knowledge of herb and plant lore that made him a great healer. His god-man part gave him the knowledge of spirit. He knew well also the balance of the masculine and feminine energies, for he was educated by Apollo, the sun, and Artemis, the moon. Thus he was instilled with great wisdom and was given the job of initiating the youth of Greek nobility into spiritual values and respect for divine law.

One day he was visited by his friend Heracles who had just come from slaying the Hydra. Unfortunately some of

Heracles' arrows were still contaminated with deadly poison from one of the Hydra's many snaky heads, and he accidentally wounded Chiron in the thigh with one of them. Just as there is a healing power in snake venom, there is perhaps a similar potency hidden in the Hydra's deadly poison. The Hydra was a hideous water monster who lived in the unfathomable Lernaean swamps, said to be the source of several different rivers. Water, especially unfathomably deep water, is an ancient symbol of the unconscious through which flow all the energies of life as well as the bubbling springs of the emotions, particularly grief. So this might indicate the depth of experience that Chiron acquired through his wound. As an immortal Chiron could not die, and was therefore left to live his life with the pain and the power of the poison. His time was spent in teaching spiritual wisdom and in healing. He has become known as the Wounded Healer, and as the ancient Greek saying goes, *only the wounded physician heals*. Like Parsifal, this legend illustrates the gains that can come from using life's wounds wisely. This gives me hope.

So now I realised that I must not bury any of the new awareness I had gained over the last years, but I must integrate it so that it could be used consciously in relationship to any woman I might meet in the future, to my Self, and ultimately to the Beloved.

There was once a lover who had sighed for long years in separation from his beloved, and wasted in the fire of remoteness. From the rule of love, his heart was empty of patience, and his body weary of his spirit; he reckoned his life without her as a mockery, and time consumed him away. How many a day he found no rest in longing for her; how many a night the pain of her kept him from sleep; his body was worn to a sigh, his heart's wound had turned him to a cry of sorrow. He had given a thousand lives for one taste of the cup of her presence, but it availed him not. The doctors knew no cure for him, and companions avoided his company; yea, physicians have no medicine for one sick of love, unless the favour of the beloved one deliver him.

At last, the tree of his longing yielded the fruit of despair, and the fire of his hope fell to ashes. Then one night he could live no more, and he went out of his house and made for the market place. On a sudden, a watchman followed after him. He broke into a run, with the watchman following; then other watchmen came together, and barred every passage to the weary one. And the wretched one cried from his heart, and ran here and there, and moaned to himself: 'Surely this watchman is 'Izra'il, my angel of death, following so fast upon me, or he is a tyrant of men, seeking to harm me.' His feet carried him on, the one bleeding with the arrow of love, and his heart lamented. Then he came to a garden wall, and with untold pain he scaled it, for it proved very high; and forgetting his life, he threw himself down to the garden.

And there he beheld his beloved with a lamp in her hand, searching for a ring she had lost. When the heart-surrendered lover looked on his ravishing love, he drew a great breath and raised up his hands in prayer, crying; 'O God! Give Thou glory to the watchman, and riches and long life. For the watchman was Gabriel, guiding this poor one; or he was Israfil, bringing life to this wretched one!'

Indeed, his words were true, for he had found many a secret justice in the seeming tyranny of the watchman, and seen how many a mercy lay hid behind the veil. Out of wrath, the guard had led him who was athirst in love's desert to the sea of his loved one, and lit up the dark night of absence with the light of reunion. He had driven one who was afar, into the garden of nearness, had guided an ailing soul to the heart's physician.

Now if the lover could have looked ahead, he would have blessed the watchman at the start, and prayed on his behalf, and he would have seen that tyranny as justice; but since the end was veiled to him, he moaned and made his plaint in the beginning. Yet those who journey in the garden of knowledge, because they see the end in the beginning, see peace in war and friendliness in anger.

From the Valley of Knowledge in 'The Seven Valleys.'
Baha'u'llah

ELEVEN

Lifeline

I went out to the hazel wood
Because a fire was in my head
And cut and peeled a hazel wand
And hooked a berry to a thread;
And when white moths were on the wing
And moth-like stars were flickering out
I dropped the berry in a stream
And caught a little silver trout.

When I had laid it on the floor
I went to blow the fire aflame
But something rustled on the floor
And someone called me by my name:
It had become a glimmering girl
With apple blossom in her hair
Who called me by my name and ran
And faded through the brightening air.

Though I am old from wandering
Through hollow lands and hilly lands,
I will find out where she came from
And kiss her lips and take her hands:
And walk among long dappled grass,
And pluck till time and times are done
The silver apples of the moon,
The golden apples of the sun.

W. B. Yeats
'The Song of Wandering Aengus'

In my days of solitude on the moors, I would jog regularly in the mornings. One of my routes took me high up on to the moors, and I would always stop there for a while to meditate. The view was stunning. I could see all of the Lothians stretching thirty miles west towards Edinburgh which huddled around the volcanic mound of Arthur's Seat and the Castle. On a good day, beyond them, I could see Ben Lomond some seventy-five miles off. To the north was Treprain Law, Berwick Law, the Bass Rock, and the wide expanse of The Firth of Forth with May Island and the Paps of the Kingdom of Fife beyond. To the east was the cold North Sea, and to the south the Lammermuir hills leading away to the Borders. It is said to be an area of powerful ley lines which doesn't surprise me at all considering the magnetic pull of all those volcanic and granite lumps by which I was surrounded.

A mile or so away on a raised plateau circled by a deep ditch and home to a few war-torn Scots pine, was the ancient site of a Roman Camp. It is totally exposed to the elements and must have been a dreaded posting for soldiers from the southern climes, but as a strategic vantage point for the region it was unbeatable. Way below, immersed in a wooded glen, was the Goblin's Haw, an underground hall with deep dungeons beneath the ruins of a castle worthy of any Grail legend or Tolkien saga.

My head was buzzing with the stories I had been reading about adepts and masters in the writings of Paul Brunton, Yogananda, Wellesley Tudor Pole, and Spalding's 'Masters of the Himalayas.' These authors gave first hand accounts of how such wise beings had appeared to them as if out of nowhere, given them blessings and some much needed advice, and then disappeared again. They always experienced the adepts as totally normal and substantial human beings, and it was only after the event that they realised they had been in the presence of something paranormal.

The stories told that an adept might as easily appear to them at home at their writing desk as on the side of some remote Himalayan peak. The experiences were always transformational, for an adept is a being who has mastered as it were the process of turning base metal into gold, an alchemist. I always have trouble believing these accounts told by other people however much I trust them. I need firsthand experience, and I longed for such a meeting myself. I desperately needed a guide, a teacher.

These mornings, sitting on my special rock, the rising sun warm on my back, I would look at these magnificent views to the North and the West, close my eyes and pray for the teacher to come my way. He never did. Perhaps I was simply facing the wrong direction, for don't teachers normally appear in the East? Then one morning I had a lovely story drop into my mind, out of the blue as I sat there, told to me by a soft friendly male voice.

A middle-aged man, who was searching for meaning and torn by the circumstances of his life, climbed a tall hill. He prayed all the while that he might find a master sitting on top of the hill who would help him and advise him about his place in the world. When he eventually reached the summit he found that he was completely alone on the great hill.

One thing he was learning on his journey was patience, so he decided not to despair. He looked around and chose a suitable rock to sit upon. He sat down, crossed his legs like an Indian yogi, closed his eyes and awaited whatever might be. Many hours passed, many thoughts entered his mind, and hunger gnawed at his belly. But patiently he waited and gradually the waters of his mind ceased to move and all was still, inside and out.

Days passed, months passed, and still no-one came. As the years passed he grew older and greyer whilst he waited for his master. His hunger was long forgotten and sometimes he even forgot why he was there at all.

Then one day, being by now very sensitive to every cell inside of himself as well as to every atom in the universe outside of himself, he felt a movement, as if a long way off a pebble had been thrown into his still lake. Gently he opened his eyes and came out of his eternity.

Far in the distance, way down in the valleys, he saw a figure coming towards him. It was then that he remembered why he was there, and he thought to himself, 'At last my master is coming.' And his heart, which had almost stopped in the still lake of his meditation, began to pick up rhythm and it beat faster and faster the closer the figure came.

Soon he could see some details in the features of the man who was coming up towards him. He was young, weather beaten and handsome, with an earnest look in his eye. The old man began to feel a little self-conscious of the rags he wore and his unkempt grey hair and beard, ravaged by the years of changing seasons. But he sat there and waited, and tried to remember all the questions he had wanted so desperately to ask his master when he had first arrived at the summit all that time ago. But his mind was empty of all questions.

By now the beautiful young man was so close that the old man could hear his heaving breath as he made his final assent to the top of the hill. He arrived, and smiling with relief, looked deep into the eyes of the old man. They stayed staring into each others eyes for a long time, and there was a strange sense of recognition between them. The old man was struggling to find words, embarrassed that after all this time and in the presence of the one for whom he had been waiting he could think of nothing to say. But then, just as he was about to break the silence with some gesture of welcome, the young man spoke:

'Master,' he said as he dropped his head in respect to the old man, 'I am so relieved to find you at last on this hill, I have travelled so many years to find you. Please bless me Master!'

Adepts and teachers do not always come to us the way that we might expect.

In November 1994, just after the end of my relationship with Lucy, I had a dream that was the start a whole process destined to carry me further along the path of relationship to my anima.

I have just re-sat my driving test, and I am on my way back to a large car park to collect my car. There I have arranged to meet Karin who has been in contact saying that she wants to meet up with me. The car park is on a steep incline away from me, and my car is down towards the bottom. Some way from the car stands my mother, my sister, and my girlfriend with whom I have recently ended, she resembles Lucy but is called Gale. Standing by the open passenger door of the car is Karin. I am so excited to see her, and she comes running up the hill towards me. She has aged somewhat, but I still find her beautiful. She is a little distressed, swollen and red in the face. She says something to me (I cannot recall what) *but I reply by reassuring her that everything is fine because now we can spend all the time in the world together. Now Gale comes over with my mother and my sister, and in an uninhibited and joyful way I introduce them all to Karin. All of them, even Gale, are very happy to meet Karin and for me to have re-passed my driving test. I am so delighted to see Karin again because I know that I can help her, and it feels as if I am meeting something long lost in myself.*

The dream seemed very encouraging. In her book 'Addiction to Perfection', Marion Woodman talks about how all the oppressive and negative archetypal feminine figures congregate around the mother complex. Here though the mood felt positive, my mother was nurturing and the female figures gathered about seemed happy and healthy, all save Karin, anima, who had come to me for help. The *gale* with Lucy was over and she too was happy. Lastly, I had re-passed my driving test. So it seemed to me that for the meantime I had passed the tests of the dragon battles with the mother complex, the devouring mother, the Hideous Damsel, the witch, all perhaps one and the same. I knew too that I could heal the anima, and that I had all the time in the world to do so. Now my anima and I could get into my car, the vehicle which carries me, i.e. my body, and drive off up the road of life together.

My next training was with Gerda Boyesen in a body-oriented psychotherapy she calls Biodynamics. It is a therapy in which emotional repression, trauma, and the like is accessed and eased through attention to the body. We learn how to move, contain and exit the energies in the body. The training took the form of twelve committed people who met regularly every six weeks for a long weekend during which we practised new techniques, and discovered yet more about ourselves. Gerda believes Carl Jung's maxim that *no one can take his patient further than he has been himself,* so knowing oneself is as important as knowing the techniques and theories.

She suggests that working in such a group is like Greek theatre, meaning that for each individual the other members of the group can become outwardly tangible aspects of his/her own psyche. Group work therefore is an opportunity to work consciously with other people as objects in the Freudian sense. (The object is someone or something in the outside world, e.g. the mother, on to whom the individual projects inner qualities, positive or negative). This was particularly pertinent for me. In the group and amongst the trainers were mother figures, father figures, sisters, brothers, witches, magicians, and wise fools, and with their co-operation and permission it was a way for me relate to these aspects of myself.

There were two young women in the group who enabled me to work very closely with my anima, or what

241

Robert A. Johnson calls the double anima. In our monogamous society it is usually impossible, if one abides by convention, to interact in an uninhibited way with these two aspects of double anima.

The two anima figures generally represent the light and dark sides of man's capacity for appreciating the feminine. The light anima is often idealistic, lofty, noble, ascetic; the dark anima is a gypsy, illicit, wildly sensuous, chaotic .... If one brings this best discipline (i.e. monogamy) to bear on the subject, his unlived anima is likely to languish and go negative or die and leave the man lifeless in middle age. Or if one follows the current trend and lets his anima rule his life without bringing discipline to her, he probably will fall into the chaos that is so common in relationship today. An ideal solution is to marry a woman who bears one of a man's anima images and invest the other in an art or creative endeavour in his outer life. It is one of the large cultural tasks facing us in our age to find a creative solution to the double anima in a man.

Robert A. Johnson. 'Lying with the Heavenly Woman'

So here I was again with a heaven-sent opportunity to explore the wisdom of what I was reading, this time from within the safety of our group.

Both women came from Norway. Liv was the fair, blue-eyed, innocent light anima of the heavens reminiscent of Karin; Line was the dark gypsy anima of the earth. Liv was very self-contained, she seemed to know herself well, and my interaction with her in the year preceding the following incidents was quite distant, although my heart would pound as she resonated with the Karin in me. We sort of walked around each other. Line, on the other hand, was far more in touch with her sensuality, and when we worked together in group exercises there was always a strong sexual charge between us, and this, I discovered, was quite mutual.

So both women animated me in different ways, one from the ideal realms of the heavens, the other from the sensual realms of the earth. I felt very close to them both and prayed for an opportunity to converse with them directly as anima, like a piece of Greek theatre. This would be up to me to instigate, and as in the school dance I would have to have the courage to make the first move and face possible rejection.

The opportunity came at the end of a workshop in February 1995. One of the trainers had been to see the new version of The Jungle Book, and had said to me that I reminded her of Mowgli. I felt quite flattered by this, but thought that it would be a good idea to go and see the film for myself to check out what she meant. I spontaneously asked Liv and Line if they would like to come with me, and they thought it was a great idea. I felt like a spoilt sugar daddy sitting between them during the movie, as they were only half my age. Mowgli was a strong, intuitive young man who learned all the wisdom of the jungle, he would undoubtedly make a fine animus figure for any woman. Still, I remained flattered by the trainer's projections, and somehow it made me feel a little more confident to be up to the task of talking things out with these two beautiful young women. I felt that, as with the trainer, it was very likely that I was holding forms of animus projection for them too.

After the movie we went for a bite to eat, and Liv and

Line suggested that I accompany them to a jazz pub in the Portobello Road that they often frequented when they were in London. I had often wondered where they disappeared to in the evenings. Pubs and clubs had been off my agenda for years whilst I had withdrawn into myself to do the inner work, they were the antithesis of the solitude and quiet that I had found it necessary to seek out. But around these two I felt full of energy again and gratefully accepted their offer, hoping that sometime during the evening I would have the courage to talk to them both about the Greek theatre idea.

The pub was loud and smoky, but above the din I started to explain to them how I projected anima on to them both. Neither of them had heard of the concept of anima and animus, so I explained it to them. They were both very intrigued, and they willingly entered the play. The three of us started to be very honest about the feelings we had for each other, and as we let down our defences we entered a realm of reality that always feels more like home to me. No longer were we having to abide by the rules of the convention, where we would be feeling one thing and saying another from the safety of the masks we wore to protect ourselves in the world.

I told them about Karin and how Liv was carrying those projections for me. I told Line how my energies were raised when I was around her, but that what I really felt towards her was the kind of care and protection a father feels towards his daughter. Liv had learned to contain her feelings so strongly that she couldn't really say how she felt about me, she said that she liked to appear sweet and innocent, but knew that inside were buried far darker feelings that she had never dared to look at. She was in a relationship and had a young daughter who kept her very busy, giving her little opportunity to delve into her inner world. The time was not yet right. I had no desire to destabilise her relationship, and I wanted to be clear about this. Early on we confided that neither of us was the one the other was looking for, though we were well suited to do this work together.

Line was initially upset at being felt as my daughter, and said she was now a little jealous of her friend Liv. She said that the raw libido energy that passed between us in the group sometimes had made her confused, but that talking about it now, and us both owning up to it, had dissipated some of that confusion. The father/daughter situation was no coincidence. Line's parents had split up when she was young and she had had to live with her neurotic and abusive mother. Her father was her rock through her teenage years and as a consequence she adored him, often feeling jealous toward his girlfriends. Some of this was projected on to me and I was very pleased that we had discovered the mutual ground where we could be of service to each other.

For my part, I wondered what it meant to be feeling so fatherly towards her, yet to also feel this surge of energy. I soon realised that my own daughters were just entering their teenage years, one was twelve and the other thirteen, and that the gift Line gave me was that I was being made aware of the unconscious sexual energy that often passes between daughter and father during these years. I would never want to abuse my daughters physically or emotionally, and my chats with Line have helped me understand the distortions that can arise, whilst making me aware of the healthy place a father has in his daughter's life.

I love to hug my daughters and kiss them good night or good-bye, I believe these are the kinds of things a father can give his daughters that allows them a healthy relationship with the masculine; but there is a fine line between too much and too little physical contact, and it is necessary for a father to be aware of this. A normal father/daughter relationship is self governing, in that most daughters go through a stage of not wanting physical contact with their fathers, and not wanting to be seen dead with them in the street. It's a sort of love/hate relationship. The psychologist Donald Winnicott suggested that daughters usually go through a stage of hating their fathers, and that it is the father's job to recognise this and to not run away, so that the daughter sees that being angry doesn't lead to being abandoned by the masculine. Most fathers do not feel sexual towards their daughters, but it is well worth being aware that this can happen.

A triangle was developing between the three of us, and rich soil was being tilled. The night was still young when the pub shut, and Liv suggested we all go to a club around the corner. It was a dingy West Indian dive, a kind of basement café with torn plastic bench seats, and the only dance space was in the narrow aisle between them. The base line of the music thumped off the flaking walls into the tiny space, and ganja smoke clouded the air. At the table in front of us a couple smooched quietly. Across the aisle a lonely Irishman sat cadging cigarettes and rolling joints which he chain-smoked.

We three huddled happily together and continued our

chat. I drank Coke, while the two women drank beer and smoked, but this caused no disconnection between us as was often the case with me when others around me started to drink too much. Behind was a small bar where some of Liv's West Indian friends sat gossiping, and in a cramped booth the DJ moved snakily to his music. Sitting at our backs was an older West Indian man whom I began to realise was taking more than a passing interest in us.

After about an hour, he could no longer resist coming over to talk. He leant down resting his elbows on our table, and eased his pleasant face into our little triangle. It was as if he spoke a different language, and I could barely make out what he was saying, other than that he bore the unlikely name of Antonio. As I began to pick up the gist of it, I realised that the foreignness was more in the content of what he was saying than in the way he spoke. He was talking only of energy, and the huge energy that he saw passing between the three of us, and he kept saying that it was very selfish to be keeping all that energy to ourselves, and that we should dance and share it out into the room. Then he did something that I shall never forget. He stared into my eyes with such intensity that I felt a twinge of fear and, without warning, he thrust his right index finger deep into my solar plexus whilst his husky West Indian voice bellowed,

'Act-i-vate yourself man, act-i-vate yourself!'

The energy went straight into me as in unison I rose up with Line and began a dance that was so sensual that even Antonio seemed surprised. He roared with pleasure and laughter as we danced on and on, encouraging us to dance as long into the night as we could. Later he was so pleased at the way we had shared out our energy that he wanted to drive us all home free of charge in his minicab. With that one simple poke of the finger, this most unlikely and unexpected adept, this Afro-Caribbean taxi driver, had pointed to what was lacking in me. I had to become aware of the immense energy that I held inside myself and I had to channel it and share it in appropriate ways. Yes it is sexual, but it is also spiritual. Erotic feeling is equatable with religious intensity. I realised that from then on as best I could I had to live it, to feel it, and to channel it into everything I did, and that this was to live authentically.

That night we returned to the room in which the group worked and I lay for a few hours between these two heavenly women. It was physically innocent, but spiritually profound. They nestled into my chest as I stroked their hair and sang a long string of songs to them. Later the songs became American Indian chants I knew, and then they became chants I had never known before. I sank into a deep contentment, and became the protective warrior lying with his two loving squaws. But all things must pass, and on hearing a clock strike four somewhere outside, I decided to get up and walk back to where I was staying before I too dozed off and risked being awakened by the cleaner in the morning.

The streets were deserted and only a sad old tramp broke the silence, wheeling his supermarket trolley through the night. I played with the names of the two women as I ambled along. Liv, I knew, meant 'life.' As anima, she represented the activating force that could bring me back into life; but what of Line? I thought the most obvious interpretation was that the name, though pronounced Lina, suggests 'line'; and yes, she had thrown me a line that reactivated my life-force. When I got back to my friends' house I crept silently up to my bedroom, but sleep didn't come easily so I began to write a poem. When I had finished it, I decided to put their names together as the title, and it was only then that I saw that the combination of their two names said, LIFELINE. How amazing! What gifts I was getting. Yes, the two of them had thrown me a lifeline. The Concise Oxford Dictionary describes lifeline as 'the sole means of communication' which begs the change to 'soul' means of communication. Webster's defines it thus: 'something regarded as indispensable for the maintaining or protection of life.' These two women, bless their loving hearts, were helping me survive.

LIFELINE

I recall the clock
Strike four outside
Like coyote howling
To the full moon.

I deftly left the bed
Using muscles I still had
My two silent muses sleeping
Light and dark, dark and light.

Weaving through streets
Laced in dreamers' dreams

In awe of my luck
The gift of Life and Line.

In the cushioned night
A rusty squeaking grows
A piss-stained tramp with twisted trolley
Limps crab like by.

As his numb solitude
Fades into the night towards nowhere
What glory it is to be able to feel
And to be given the chance to see.

Not for I to sleep on Alpha
And to wake on Omega
Only to be mystified
By the veiled letters in between.

Goethe said *all things are metaphors,* and this suggests to me that everything that happens in life can help to give it meaning. The more I became aware of what was happening to me, the more I realised that every detail of my life was indeed yielding meaning. Life is supremely economic and nothing is wasted, all we have to do is pay attention to it.

After my time in London with Liv and Line, I returned to the North to deal with the sale of my house and studio. It was now the Spring of 1995 and Jessica, Robert and the children had moved out of the house the year previously to a lovely mill farm a few miles down the road, and meantime we had rented it out for a year, as we were unable to sell it due to the recession. I had moved out of the little flat in dogshit alley because the owner wanted it back for herself, but the rent I was receiving from our house enabled me to look for a place with an additional bedroom, which would make it easier to have the children when they came. I had taken the first rental I came across as I had little time for house hunting. I was steeped in practical and theoretical exams for a qualification I needed for my Biodynamics training.

I needed to qualify as a masseur, and the only place I could find to teach me locally was an old-fashioned beauty school in the centre of Edinburgh. Looking back, it was all pretty comical really, but my life was still in chaos at the time. I was right in the midst of the transition from the known old life to the unknown new life, which included this attempt at a career change.

I will never forget walking up the hill one morning towards the beauty school, clutching my Safeways bag full of note books and strange massage lotions, when my mobile phone rang. This was the street I had driven up so many times in my swanky V8 cars in my more affluent days as a well-to-do photographer, and here I was now feeling broke and under constant pressure to find the cash to pay for next month's aliment and all my other basic living expenses, whilst trying to pass these difficult exams.

It was a man from Scotland's leading media magazine whom I thought was trying to sell me advertising space, so I tried to give him short shrift as there was no way I could afford such a thing. He interrupted me to tell me that his magazine had just done a survey in the advertising industry to create a league table of Scotland's photographers, and that I had been voted number one by a huge majority. The irony made me chuckle, 'if they could only see me now.'

Eventually we did manage to sell our house, and it was a great relief to know that at last I would have some money to buy a small place of my own. At that very same time the owner of the place I was renting wanted to sell, and I made her an offer which she immediately accepted. It suited both of us during these depressed times. The worst part of the sale of our big house was that I would have to clear all my stuff out of the attic and studio. I had hardly seen the place in the last four years, as it caused me enormous pain to go near it. It was a reminder of a past that had vanished, and a present and future that would never be. However, there was no avoiding this final visit.

With the help of two friends I filled two huge removal lorries. One load went to the rubbish dump, and the other went to a friend's farm for storage. Amongst all the stuff was an old gun case which I had kept since my student days, and it had lain dormant in all the attics of all my houses over the last twenty years. In it were items of sentimental value from those times: school reports, cricket caps, old photographs and love letters. This was the only thing I took back to my little house.

In it were several of Karin's letters written to me whilst we were both still at school, and I found photographs I had taken of her a few years later at college when I was an aspiring photographer and she an aspiring model. Why had I kept this stuff all these years? As I savoured the letters and gazed at the photographs, it began to dawn on me that maybe I still had it all so that it might have some meaning for me right now. All this stuff had been there above my head in the attic all these years, whilst the fortunes of my life rose and fell, patiently awaiting this moment. To clear out my attic was to do justice to the memories that my mind still carried. It was all very symbolic.

I realised that I would have to do honour to this stuff, I would have to go through it and make some sense of it. I bought a large scrapbook, and devoted an entire week to entering this dormant world and bringing it back to life. I cut out the photographs and reread the letters, littering the floor with all these old memories. I made blow ups of the photographs, and I stuck twenty-year-old Karin's life-size face to the walls. Stocking up with food and locking my front door, I dived into this other world, searching for meaning. For a whole week I lived, ate, dreamed, and dialogued with my anima.

I started to piece it all together by sticking her words and her photographs into the scrapbook, writing my own dialogue alongside. I began it with an American Indian love song that Lucy had given to me.

I know not whether you have been absent
I lie down with you
I rise up with you
In my dreams you are with me.
If my ear drops tremble within my ears
I know it is you moving within my heart.

The photographs I had taken of her back in 1972 had never been used for anything. Now, twenty-three years on, they seemed incredibly relevant. It was as if something in me back then knew that I was taking the pictures for this future purpose. I had taken them on Hampstead Heath in the early autumn of that year which, as it happened, was the year in which both Liv and Line had been born. Karin wore a beautiful white cheesecloth dress, and with the sun breaking through the trees behind her, the outline of her beautiful dancer's body could be seen through the semi-transparent material. I had photographed her as the unattainable goddess she was to me. As I described earlier in the book, in one of her letters she wrote:

I'm far from being a goddess, my love! I guess there are a great many things which I should explain to you --- I will some day but at the moment I don't really understand myself --- you know me --- Chaos!

Nov. 1967

Yes .... Chaos: the goddess representing the primeval void from which evolved Erebus, Tartarus, and Eros: Night, The Underworld, and Desire. Order in the universe was created out of the formless and jumbled mass of Chaos. Some wisdom in Karin knew she was bringing these things to me, but I couldn't see her as Chaos in those days, I needed to see her as a gilded princess, a romantic love, untouchable to me. I spoke to her in the scrapbook.

'I never touched your breasts, I never lit your fire. I was just a boy, just a

boy. But through these years, this passage of time, you have taught me well.'

I asked her, 'Why did you come to me then?'

She replied, 'To break your heart wide open, so that you could live and feel life to the full.'

'And why do you come back to me now?'

'So that you can see me properly for the first time, and so that you can reclaim that part of yourself, your ANIMA, your SOUL, your CREATIVITY. I am no longer that, I am a woman, and I can and I will speak to you.'

I found a few lines of a poem I had written to her.

I wrote your name on a pebble
And threw it into the sea
Asking Neptune to send you
Spinning back to me.

And so he had.

In another picture I had got her to lie down on the ground and covered her in dead leaves, and she lay there, eyes closed like Sleeping Beauty. I pasted it into the scrapbook and wrote,

Kiss her and she will reawaken. The briars have opened up before me, and the path is clear to the place she lies. I have been away slaying dragons, and now I return to the castle, through the tangled woods to kiss her and bring her, her in me, back to life. Circumambulating her is such sublime anticipation; the best meal I shall ever eat. I watch her, she is perfection. I will put a mirror to her nose to see if she still breathes. Her heart has slowed right down. All these years she has not moved, time has stood still for her, her in me. So much energy, libido, prana, life-force, sexual power, lying there dormant. I touch her gently on her raised hip like a wren landing ... She is not cold. She maintains life. Her hair smells of the sweet earth, her perfume is heaven, her skin is silk. I will kiss her back to life. Awake princess! Awake!

All this time you have been asleep in me. I shall carry you now wherever I go, into and through whatever worlds I am to travel: you are part of me, you are the fire that I, the man, must kindle. You are the Aphrodite in my heart and I come all the way through to you, all the way through you. Yes, of course you were hazy and dozy because I put no wood on your fire, I did nothing to clear the air around you, I was not clear. Now, I hold my lance out and clear away the thorns - the rose briars - and I seek to raise you, my sleeping beauty.
I want to WAKE YOU UP!   I want to ACT-I-VATE YOU!

This felt like an intensely sacred experience, and as I prayed for more guidance, I opened the 'Writings of Baha'u'llah' and read the following, which describes how the Word of God came to Baha'u'llah through a *Maiden from Heaven* when, in 1852, he had been thrown into the infamous black dungeon of Tehran, the Siyah-Chal, by the Shah, for being a threat to the Moslem authorities.

During the days I lay in the prison of Tehran, though the galling weight of the chains and the stench-filled air allowed me but little sleep, still in those infrequent moments of slumber I felt as if something flowed from the crown of my head over my breast, even as a mighty torrent that precipitateth itself upon the earth from the summit of a lofty mountain. Every limb of My body would, as a result, be set afire. At such moments My tongue reciteth what no man could bear to hear.

From 'The Epistle to the Son of the Wolf'

According to the scriptures we are all made in the image of God, and therefore there is no reason why our own experience, albeit on a smaller scale, cannot be compared to those of the great prophets, and I think Baha'u'llah was telling me so. With the lifeline thrown to me by Liv and Line I had returned to Scotland to clear out my attic, and by paying attention to the metaphorical details that life had put my way, I had reached into the source of my being where I could activate myself and become reanimated into a fully creative being.

To complete my scrap-book I decided to match to scale a contemporary picture of myself to one of Karin's. I then cut it out and pasted it on to Karin's picture, and there we were side by side in the woods, the perfect couple. Before me was illustrated the sum of my life's work thus far. The mystical marriage of the masculine and feminine, *coniunctio* to the alchemists. It had taken me twenty-three years to become man enough for her, and now I could see how right we looked together.

Excited by the new feelings of connection generated by the work I had done, and temporarily forgetting the mythological level I had been operating on, I became a little literal and decided to write Karin a letter. I sent it to her last known address which was her mother's flat in Belsize Park,

257

London. It was there that I had last seen her twenty-three years previously, just before I got married to Jessica. Not surprisingly I never received a reply, they must have moved on years ago. But less than a week later I had a simple dream.

I am with Karin, I have found her. We are lying naked, gently touching each other. I feel that we are together at last, and it is a sublime feeling of union. And she says to me, simply, 'I have received your letter.'

So what I tried to shift outside my own psyche by trying to contact her in the flesh, was deftly shifted back inside by the wisdom of the unconscious, and thus it was kept where it belonged. The job seemed to be complete. We may well meet again one day, I would be fascinated, but the main thing is that the inner work was realised.

My reconnection to the effect that Karin has had on my life helped make clear something that had always occurred in my relationships. In my marriage and in every other relationship that I had ever experienced there always came a time when I would feel trapped. I realised now that I had given my heart to Karin as a teenager, and because I had projected my whole inner feminine on to her, it was inconceivable that I could ever give my heart to anyone else. I was fundamentally unavailable. Unconsciously my heart would always be saying, 'This isn't her, this isn't the one you promised yourself to; I can't be intimate with this one, let's get out of here!' But by reclaiming my anima as a part of myself, by withdrawing the projection, as Jung puts it, I now stood a chance of being a more complete person, a man who knew far more about his feminine side, and hopefully more capable of having a healthy relationship should the opportunity ever arise again.

TOMORROW

And tomorrow the sun will shine again
And on the path that I follow
It will reunite us, the blessed ones
Amidst the sun-breathing world.
And to the shore, broad and blue with the waves
We shall go down quietly and slowly.
Mute, we shall look into each other's eyes,
And upon us will descend the great
Silence of happiness.

John Henry Mackay

TWELVE

Walking through walls

> A big revolution is to come now.
> This civilisation is spent up.
> It cannot give happiness to people.
> It will be removed.
>
> Shivapuri Baba. 'The Long Pilgrimage'

A few months after the walls of the Eastern Bloc came tumbling down I was touring various cities in what was still known then as Czechoslovakia. I had been asked to give some talks on the story of what had happened to me in the Himalayas. In the city of Brno I met a young man called Daniel who had an intriguing tale to tell. He told me that his father had been a prominent communist party member who ran one of the biggest factories in the city. His father was very frightened of losing his position, and would not allow Daniel to do anything controversial that might reflect on him and thus jeopardise it. As a consequence Daniel had never been into a church, and knew nothing about the stranger who hung on a cross there.

All through his mid teens Daniel was restlessly looking for something to fill what he called the 'empty space' inside himself. He went as often as he could to discos, and began drinking heavily. He soon found however that this gave him only temporary satisfaction, so he decided to try something else. He joined a gym and started to work out. Although this was more healthy, it also fell short of the sort of satisfaction he was seeking. He was looking for the kind of ecstasy that can only be found in genuine spirit.

> *Where did I come from and what am I supposed to be doing?*
> *I have no idea .... my soul is from elsewhere*
> *I'm sure of that, and I intend to end up there.*
> *This drunkenness began in some other tavern:*
> *When I get back around to that place*
> *I'll be completely sober ......*
> *What is the soul? ..... I cannot stop asking.*
> *If I could taste one sip of an answer*
> *I could break out of this prison for drunks.*
> *I didn't come here of my own accord*
> *And I can't leave that way*
> *Whoever brought me here will have to take me home.*
>
> *Rumi*

When Daniel was seventeen years old communism in

the Soviet bloc had begun to collapse, and it was then that I met him. He had never been abroad and, as soon as the walls of communism had crumbled, he used his limited resources to take a train over to West Germany to see what the West looked like. He could only afford to stay there for twenty-four hours, but whilst waiting for a train home he met two evangelistic Christians on the platform. He spent five hours talking to them and was absolutely agog when they revealed to him the meaning of the man hanging on the cross and the concept of God. He said he had felt dizzy as he began to feel his empty space filling up. Literally in high spirits, he returned to Brno totally electrified by these new ideas. On his way home from the station he bumped into some Baha'is at a bookstall who also seemed to have some fresh ideas about how God expressed himself into the world. Daniel couldn't believe what was happening to him, and by the time he got home from his trip to the West his spiritual cup was overflowing. At last it felt like this was the real nourishment he had been looking for these last years. By the time I met him he had become a Baha'i.

It is the nature of the human being to search for meaning during the teenage years. In tribal society it was always the time of initiation, the time when youths would be separated from parents and tribe to be initiated by knowledgeable elders. Without such eldership in our culture there is no conscious initiation, so our children are forced to go out and seek the fire of spirit for themselves and they have to make their own mistakes. They are feeling an empty space inside themselves that demands to be filled because it is ravenously hungry. This is what the teenagers' desire for excess is all about, and more often than not all they end up finding is false spirit: drink, drugs, clubbing, risky sports, driving at reckless speeds, the need to separate themselves from their parent's generation at all costs.

I believe what they are seeking is God. By God I don't mean the old man with a grey beard who sits up in the clouds proclaiming judgment on each individual. I mean the awesome power behind the universe, the unknowable creative force which the American Indians call the Great Spirit, and it is infinitely more sublime than any drug or false spirit. Teenagers want to feel whole, but today our culture has so many consumables on offer that, as with the old joke about Chinese food, however much they stuff themselves with they soon feel hungry again. More often than not they fail in their search and the craving ends up getting buried beneath the more mundane concerns of work, money, marriage, children, and the sheer slog of day-to-day survival. Sooner or later however the pangs of hunger will probably re-emerge, and this is often what triggers a mid-life crisis.

I have always been suspicious of people who, including myself, become religious in later life. I wonder what it is they are after. Is the emptiness and the hunger they feel merely a desire to be rescued and to return to the symbiotic ecstasy of the womb? Is it a relapse towards the comfort of mama's apron strings? Is it an avoidance of facing some psychological problem caused in childhood? Is it fear? Are they scared of death, or frightened of being alone? Or is it a genuine need to seek spiritual fulfilment and a community of like minds? Daniel's story helped persuade me that it could be the latter, for it demonstrated that there is a real space in the human heart that needs to be filled by spirit. Brought up as a communist with no spiritual instruction, his psyche had not been tainted by religious brainwashing as a child. In his driven search he had acknowledged the empty space within himself, and had tried unsuccessfully to fill it with worldly things, but when the time was right he found the nourishment he was really after. He had made his own way into the forest and come to the spiritual life unpolluted by conditioning.

Another point of view which I like a lot, is proposed by James Hillman in 'The Soul's Code'. In it he suggests that life makes much better sense when you view it in reverse: that the full-grown oak was always programmed into the original acorn. For instance, he suggests that without the difficult childhood experiences that tempered Winston Churchill's destiny, we would never have had the great wartime leader. He talks about the famous Spanish matador Manolete, who as a child was a real mama's boy and would always be cowering around her ankles, as if to compensate for an adulthood that a part of him knew would be spent in the macho world of facing fierce bulls. He also mentions his own horror of writing as a child, as if he knew that so many of his later years would be spent in filling blank pages with words. It is our own life experience that has led us to where we are today, and looking at it from the point of view of destiny, we need the events of our early lives, for better or for worse, to lead us to what our destiny wants us to become in adulthood. This is to look at life mythologically, not psychologically, for psychology only looks at life forwards, i.e. developmentally.

A good example I have observed recently comes from the remarkable story Andrew Harvey tells of his experiences with Mother Meera in his book 'Hidden Journey.' He reveals to us that as a child he absolutely adored his mother, but that at the age of six he was sent away from his home in India to a boarding school, and consequently his relationship with his mother was torn asunder, never to be the same again. This created in him a craving for mother that led him back to India as an adult where he found Mother Meera who seemed to fill the empty space.

India gave me a mother, then took her away. Years later, I found in India another Mother in another dimension, and the love I had believed lost returned. Without that first wound I would not have needed love so much or been prepared to risk everything in its search ..... From the deepest wound of my life grew its miraculous possibility.

So it was the seemingly cruel emotional history of his childhood that caused him to find the way to fill his spiritual cup in adulthood. His destiny needed the cruel history. Which comes first, psychological development or destiny? It's the old chicken and egg situation.

Filling this empty space can be a real struggle for us men. When we go inside and try to listen to our own hearts more often than not we hear a babble of other voices. When I listen the voices I most often hear are the authority figures in my life, such my father and my headmasters. Indeed all of them have threatened to become masters of my head. I have always had to decipher these conditioned responses from what my heart is really telling me. The voices are sometimes even offering some sensible advice for they are and were sensible men, and their advice is very seductive because we resonate to more or less the same conditioning. But these days there is a muffled whispering beneath their loud chattering, and it is my own voice trying to be heard above those of what Freud calls the superego. My own voice remembers the vision that I hold for my life, my golden thread, and it takes all my courage to keep this vision alive amidst the babble of oughts and shoulds coming from all those voices of authority. As we get older I think it becomes increasingly important to decipher this quiet voice within, otherwise we may die inside.

> *Don't spend your time listening to others*
> *Or other special currencies,*
> *Listen to your own heart*
> *Before   it   stops   beating.*

As if to help deal with these other voices, my career has put me in front of numerous men in pinstripe suits, headmaster type authority figures. I have photographed hundreds of executives and captains of industry, Sir This and Lord That and other Very Important Persons. I have had the privilege of glimpsing the machinations of the corporate world without having to stay and become enmeshed in it as my subjects, and my grandfathers, have chosen to be. It has become clear to me that the men in these institutions are rarely being themselves. The boardrooms are full of men whose religion is not so much initiated by the holy prophets as by profits for the shareholders, and their ethical code often gets stretched to the edge of moral decency by the pressure of having to show a profit. This habit is as old as the hills.

Custom is to them in the place of Law, and what they see done before them every day they persuade themselves may be done without sin. For customs bad in themselves seem to these men to acquire authority and prescription from the fact that they are commonly practised.

St Francis Xavier 1506-1552

This is so much so that local culture and peer pressure makes the one who stands up from the crowd and says, 'That's enough! This is not ethical,' feel sidelined, and it seriously frightens those who like to toe the company line and hold on to their jobs.

I come from a long line of successful men, and had it not been for my grandfather I could well be one of those men in suits myself, and very wealthy to boot. Over several generations, born out of the industrial revolution, my forefathers had created what became a large family business and is now a substantial public company. My grandfather sold out in 1963 for what was then a huge sum of money which he then proceeded to spend the rest of his life losing. No one really knows why he sold out, but the family myth goes that the incoming son always did battle with his father in the classic Oedipal battle, having to kill his father off as it were, and that my grandfather wished to avoid this. I have always felt it was something other than that, and I think that in a deeper sense my grandfather wanted to give his descendants a different legacy, a freedom from the yoke of a family business, a yoke to which he was tied all his life. One thing for sure is that, for better or for worse, I would certainly not be sitting here today writing this book had my grandfather not sold the business.

My father repeated this pattern in a smaller way in his business and, like my grandfather, he never seemed to enjoy what he did for a living either. However, it enabled him to afford the good things of life, to educate me and my sister privately, to live on a small farm with horses, sheep, and chickens, and a tennis court even though he didn't really play the game himself. By the time I was in my mid-thirties I had achieved most of the same things, I had a big house and I too had built a tennis court even though I didn't play the game much myself either. It was taking a long time to work these unconscious patterns out of our genes.

For the previous decade I had been making a large proportion of my very good living from helping advertise alcohol for many of the major distilleries and breweries in Scotland, and this constituted a large part of my financial success. Then after the awakening I had in my mid-thirties I gave up drinking. For a while I continued to accept these commissions and often won awards for the creative work I did, but it became more and more unacceptable for me to do it. I felt a total hypocrite. I gave up drinking not only because of the damage I felt it was doing to my own body and psyche, but because of the subtle damage the drug itself was doing to society, to the body of mankind.

My friends and business associates gave me all the good reasons for not giving up such work: 'If you don't do it someone else will,' or 'What difference does it make if one person takes a stance like this?' or 'Surely you must continue to do it to support your children.' I was called a fool by colleagues, and my wife, a non-drinker herself, considered me irresponsible. A few people understood, and I had the support of my Faith that advocates abstinence.

I was tested over and over again by circumstance. As things got tougher and tougher for me financially and I had little work, it was then that the phone would ring with the offer of a glossy and lucrative advertising campaign for some big whisky brand, tempting me back into the arena. To start with I was always riddled with guilt and doubt, but in time it got easier to say no. I was realising that I was totally alone in this, and my decision appeared to make little difference in the world other than making my family poorer, and my friends think that I was astride a very high horse. However, I became convinced that a small pebble thrown into the lake now would create a big ripple sometime later, albeit in fifty years' time maybe. I might never see the effect, but it is happening all the same. I believe it is by individuals standing their own ground, and being prepared to live by their own truth whatever it might be, that the world will change.

> *Thou canst not stir a flower*
> *Without troubling of a star.*
>
> *Francis Thompson*

In contemporary corporate jargon you don't seek a new job, you seek a new role. Like politicians, most businessmen are forced to play roles and take positions, and they need to watch their backs for fear of what might be happening somewhere outside of their control. They may appear to be arrogant but it is often only a sign of their own insecurity. The exceptions, the men with genuine power and authority, are usually relaxed and often amusing. They put on no airs and their authenticity shines through. They are in just the right place and are fulfilling their creative potential. Of course there is nothing wrong with business, only in the way it is sometimes done.

The men in suits are often the ones who have come to represent the negative aspects of the patriarchy, and they are joined now in the corporate world by women who have donned their own power suits, but that has made little difference as it is still a masculine world. Sometimes when I look through the lens of my camera into the eyes of these people I no longer see their institutionalised personas, I see the soul itself staring out at me and it often manifests as the doleful eyes of an unfulfilled child. When I get these snapshots of reality I am filled with compassion. I see the stress, I see the lost ideals, I see the lost soul, I feel the empty space.

They survive in a corporate world. *Corpus* means body, and the mother complex in me often envies the apparent security of these men who are held in the womb of their mother corporation. It is easy to expand your chest and strut about like a big lion when mama's holding arms are nearby, and mama loves to see her cubs flexing their muscles as they tumble and play. Confidence and positive thinking has become the order of the day in the business world, and you fake it until

271

you make it. 'There are no problems, only opportunities' has become the right-on jargon of the modern thrusting executive. But recession, redundancy, and insecurity have made faking it a lot harder, and over the last years mama's arms have not been quite so loving and welcoming. Many of the cubs have never lived outside the corporation and have no idea how to. They can be creative for the corporation and they can speak with the corporate voice, but they may well be dancing to a song that is utterly discordant with their own lost voice. Their safe salaries were once enough to cover a lack of creative fulfilment at work, but the insecurities brought on by the recent climate have exposed a much rawer need that is probably the real reason for the stress and the burnout. It is the need to respond to the inner voice, and it is the need to feel free of mama corporation's apron strings and papa boss's unreasonable demands.

At the end of a particularly intense period of photographing men in suits in the Spring of 1995, just after I had been thrown my lifeline, I had a long dream that not only told me something about the patriarchy, but also anticipated the work I would be doing in the near future.

I am with a man who loves peacocks. There are six male birds walking along the top of a huge wall. In addition to their coloured fans, they have the most wonderful varieties of plumage over their necks and heads in vast arrays of blacks and whites. The man says that he creates these black and white arrays himself by gently touching the birds on their necks when they are young, as a potter touches a pot on a wheel and gives it a new shape. Each one is slightly different and he is very proud of his creations.

However, impressive as they are, I feel that these birds are showpieces and that something very sinister lies behind their proud display on the wall. I rise up from ground level as if on a movie camera crane, so that I can see what is behind the wall. There I see an Auschwitz, mile upon mile of drab looking battery hen houses, and in them are caged thousands of scraggy looking female birds. It is a stark contrast to the pride of the man and his strutting peacocks.

I ask the man what he is up to. He says, 'I have to make the males big and beautiful for these six birds have to service all those thousands of caged females for breeding and making eggs. I love my creations, I'm proud of them. But I'm really frightened that if the wall breaks down all those females will swarm through and annihilate me. It's a real effort keeping that wall up, it uses so much of my energy.'

I say, 'But that is false plumage you give to the men, you manufacture that black and white stuff yourself and they have to strut up and down carrying all that excess baggage. They can only see in black and white, and it is as if they could not exist unless they wore these ridiculous black and white suits. They aren't true males, and anyway aren't they the sons and fathers of the very women whom they service? These birds aren't in their true nature, they are not wild: these males are locked into a prison of plumage, just as the females are locked into the prison of those hen houses.'

He replies, 'But I love my creation, I am the Creator!'

This makes me very angry and I say, 'You are not the Creator! You are the creator of fear, the god of the patriarchy, the god that makes false males and fears the feminine, that's who you are!'

He replies, 'I am the master of all I survey on this side of the wall, and it's safer to stay this side and keep the wall standing. If I let those females through they'll kill my six birds and they'll kill me too for what I have caused happen to them.'

273

I realise then that he is wrong, and I say, 'Your fears are unfounded. If you let the wall down those females will not murder the males, and they won't kill you either. They will have compassion for the men, after all the males are their own sons and fathers. It is in their nature that they will want to rehabilitate and care for the men. And perhaps that will mean taking off all that ridiculous black and white plumage, so that they can return to their true nature. Their natural plumage is beautiful enough, as is the females' plumage if it is allowed to develop. The females will make males of the males, so that those males can in turn make them feel truly feminine. You see, it is in their own interest to keep the male birds alive! They will not need to kill you because you will lose your power anyway, and neither the males nor the females will be interested in you any longer. There will be no more need for you, or the walls!'

The dream filled me with grief. I felt the isolation and the out-of-touchness of the men on the wall. These were not men, they were automatons. They strutted their stuff in a sort of numb ignorance, cut off from their natural wildness. It was part of me and part of most men I knew. The fact that there were six birds zeroed in on sexuality, and inferred the separation of the masculine from the life-force. The aloof position they had been forced to take by the god of fear, and the consequent degradation of the feminine to the role of battery hens, had caused a disconnection to the life-giving force of the feminine. Women are not witches to be caged and burned! If we do not take the wall down soon and consciously incorporate the healing power of the feminine, I saw that the repressed energy behind the wall might explode and we could all be in for a bad time.

The patriarchy has been composed of both men and women, and so the work involves both genders acknowledging and changing the distortions created by it. The masculine dominated god of fear has driven our society too much in his direction, and the tide of the feminist movement with their often angry voices, has rightly made this no longer tenable. Modern man is still unconsciously attached to mama. He sucks ravenously at her breast like an addict on his last cigarette. This has given rise to an unhealthy collective mother complex and made him a slave to this age of consumerism, from which he seeks his nourishment. There never seems to be enough to satisfy him and he always wants more, he is driven by the fear of scarcity. And this fear driven need is sucking mama dry, look at what he's doing to Mother Earth! Under the authority of the god of fear, and under the spell of the mother complex, he has caged the nurturing feminine and hidden her behind walls. Mother as nurturer is the healthy mother, the mother archetype, *Eve Mother of all men* as Goldmund calls her; and without mother, he says, we *cannot love* or *cannot die.* Ironically, it seems to have been the fear of the power of Mother that is the turbine that has driven the Patriarchy.

I think us men are doomed to a life dominated by fear if we do not lower our walls to allow in the feminine and have the courage to offer her sovereignty. A male dominated by fear is not really masculine at all, so the irony is that there is not enough real masculine energy around to make the feminine feel feminine. We are caught in a vicious circle. In 'Fire in the Belly' Sam Keen says,

275

.... at the present moment in history, friendship between men and women is one of the great untapped resources for renewing the world.

Without the fear, men and women would be more free to be themselves, they could celebrate their differences and unite in the wholeness shown in the Chinese symbol of yin and yang. To release the wisdom in the feminine could catalyse the masculine capacity for compassion. And I believe the beginning of this work is to start dismantling the walls.

The bricks of the walls are not only composed of fear, they contain all the elements of our hurt and our pain: grief, anger, conditional love, hate, revenge, death, abuse, prejudice, manipulation, losses of all kinds. Men and women have constructed their walls as defence mechanisms to prevent them being hurt again, and great care has to be taken in dismantling these walls. Knocking them down is counter productive. In our society it is the therapist who has the job of helping people take down these walls. The work is subtle, and unless it is done with restraint the wall might well topple down on top of the client and the therapist. By this I mean that we have learned to depend on our defences, and they are better to be dismantled brick by brick so that each brick can be seen and understood for what it is, and the purpose it has served. If the wall is demolished too quickly then the client may well be left in a complete identity crisis, or at worst a psychosis, and the therapist will have done a great disservice.

So this is where my life has led me, to the place where I am now trying to help others understand and dismantle their walls. I run workshops and retreats for people who have come to that stage of their life when their inner voice will no longer leave them alone, and they have little option but to confront their walls. The workshops are designed to help men and women deal with their unresolved fear, anger, and grief, and we have sometimes called them fittingly, 'Walking Through Walls.'

I love the work and I see it as art. The art is not in the techniques we use or the words that are spoken, but it is the creative moment when the noise on the battlefield of the workshop floor abates and, for a few moments, time is suspended as someone releases themselves from some long carried emotional burden. A brick has been taken out of the wall. It is a moment of sublime truth lost forever in time, a work of art that can never be hung on a wall, but it thrills me a lot more than any of the huge advertising hoardings I used to have dotted around our cities.

VETERANS

Suddenly we awaken
Numbly aware that we are veterans
Of some long silent war.
Children one day
Elders the next.
Possessors of a certain wisdom
Gleaned from experiences
We would never have chosen.
That same wisdom
Makes us grateful

277

For the adversities
That have sculpted our lives
As torrents carve the mountainsides.
We are moved, and we move on.

Taking down the walls makes a good metaphor for the extraordinary times into which we have been born. What is happening in the inner world of the psyche, what Mohammed called the Great War, is also happening in the outer world of nation states, what Mohammed called the Small War. The walls all have to come down sooner or later, but the chaos that can arise if a wall is taken down too quickly can be seen in what has happened in the Balkans, and the free for all that is happening in the Russian states. It shows what tensions were being held in check by the ramparts of totalitarianism, in this case communism. Now, without those walls of containment, all that repressed nationalism and free enterprise of the individual is having to be expressed, and it has erupted in uncontrollable violence, anger, greed, and corruption. Economies are wrecked, and insecurity and trauma is rife for most of the people, so much so that some wish the communists were back in power. At least with the communists they had guaranteed jobs, bread, and warm houses. It seems that this is the terrifyingly uncertain territory that has to be crossed, and we can only hope that there is some form of peace and resolution beyond.

This is absolutely equatable with what happens in therapy with the individual. As the walls are dismantled, or the dam breaks, repressed emotions of all sorts come tumbling out. There are oceans of tears, screams of murderous rage, traumas revisited. For a while it can seem like a war zone but, unlike its counterpart on the outer, it is a zone that can be held safely by the therapist. Emotion means literally 'to move out.' It is a vital movement in the body that needs to be expressed into the outside world. If we try to contain our emotions, not only are we keeping them in the wrong place, but we are stilling them when their true nature is to move. William Blake called the emotions *divine influxes*, and they are bona fide movements inside of us, and as such are sacred. So whether induced by instinct or conditioning, an emotion is nevertheless a true feeling. It resonates in our body, it is nervous impulse, it is electricity, it is vibration. We can lock it up for years, but its impulse is still there. Without attention and acknowledgement, suppressed emotions stack up inside compressing into a solid gunk, like chronic constipation, which can soak up all of the body's energy, leading to hypertension, psychic numbness, depression, and disease.

In order to remove the bricks and lift the depression, we often have to melt these buried vibrations from the place where they have been frozen in the tissues of our bodies, and this can mean the painful touching of old traumas. Like constipation, the evacuation can be just as excruciating, but once dumped there is the reward of an equally ecstatic sense of relief. Once emotions have been melted and moved through the body it is possible to leave them where they belong outside of ourselves. There they can be dispelled (de-spelled) by the clear light of day, which is consciousness, and with time and care the body can recuperate to the more fluid state it was in before the emotion or trauma became frozen inside. I believe this emotional energy finds a healthy place outside ourselves, in that Mother Nature eats it for breakfast, it is the mulch that nourishes her and she thrives on it, and she returns it to pure oxygen for our nourishment.

Nations have been raped and traumatised by history. Some nations, like our own, have been able to express themselves, and have more or less settled within their agreed boundaries. Others, who have not had the chance to express themselves because of colonisation or political oppression, have exploded into violent nationalism, or in the likes of Rwanda a reversion to violent tribalism, as their walls of containment come down. In individual therapy the walls can be deconstructed delicately, and a neurosis can be unpicked stone by stone, but in the outer world things are much coarser and for some nations the overnight break down of the walls has sometimes led to psychotic behaviour. A few, like the Czech Republic and Slovakia, have managed without bloodshed, but the news is filled with those that have not.

I am an optimist, and I believe that these are the last throes of nationalism. How long the warring factions of the world will take to establish agreed boundaries is uncertain, and who knows how long the bitterness of all the bloodshed will live on in the effected generations; but these days things have a habit of happening much more quickly than we might ever expect. Ever since that first photograph from the moon showed our little planet suspended in the vast blackness of space, a new awareness has been laid out before us, an awareness anticipated by Baha'u'llah one hundred and fifty years earlier: *the Earth is but one country, and mankind its citizens.* It is only a matter of time before we will be forced to admit how small and interdependent we all are. Sadam Hussein is a dinosaur, and the days of him and his like are numbered, but let's hope that it doesn't take another asteroid colliding with the planet to shift such negativity.

When we have established our boundaries and they are respected by others, we can let our defensive walls down, accept and relish our natural differences and co-operate in harmony. This applies as much to nations as it does to individual men and women. The vesica piscis where the circles overlap, and the *coniunctio* where the mystical marriage takes place, are arenas of great peace. When nations can meet in this way, instead of the area being a zone of conflict where mutual distrust may precipitate war, bloodshed, and the vast waste of resources that discord brings, the zone of overlap can be for trade links, aid, cultural exchange and the celebration of cultural differences. For, as in the Flower of Life, it is the overlaps that bind the whole system together.

Unfortunately, just as relationships can be held together by unhealthy codependencies instead of healthy interdependencies, so too can nations be held together by conflict. Nations have to move from codependence to interdependence, so that there is a *coniunctio* based on trust. In the meantime only a fully incorporated United Nations that lives up to its name, and has the authority to empower its decisions, can hope to keep nations out of bloodshed and expansionism.

These fruitless strifes and these pointless wars must cease,
and the Most Great Peace must come.

Baha'u'llah

A sustainable future for the body of mankind depends on each cell knowing that it is an interdependent and integral part of the whole. The health of each cell depends on the health of the whole, and the health of the whole depends upon the health of each cell. Inner city dereliction applies to both individual and state, and the question is which do we attend to first? Does attending to our inner life manifest in the healing of dereliction in the outside world, or does attending to the dereliction in the outside world result in an inner healing for the individual?

Perhaps the answer is simply to attend to both, so both can heal simultaneously.

THIRTEEN

Out of the blue sky

There is only love.
Everything else is a distortion.

One morning in a friend's cottage on the Isle of Skye I sat cross-legged on my bed immersed in my meditation practice. For several months previously I had been pondering the idea that somehow the great religions and their prophets were connected to the development of the body of mankind, which in effect is the evolution of consciousness. I felt that the body of mankind works in the same way as the individual human body: it has cells, organs, limbs, a brain, all dedicated to their various functions for the good of the whole. Individual humans I saw as the cells all working away within these functions through history for the positive evolution of the consciousness of mankind. Just as the human is kept alive by the unconscious functions of the autonomic nervous system which controls such fundamentals as heartbeat, digestion, and breathing, I felt it analogous that many individuals contribute unconsciously to the good of the body of mankind. Similarly of course, there can be cancerous cells like Adolf Hitler which threaten to destroy the body. The analogy can be stretched on and on, but the point for me was that I saw this body of mankind as being developmental like any individual human. It is an embryo, it is born, it is a child, it is an adolescent, it is an adult, it grows old and it dies or transforms. I think humankind is only just beginning to mature into adulthood.

To continue the analogy, I also saw the body of mankind as having the same seven chakras as the individual human. I had often speculated that there was a kind of metaphorical link between the prophets and the chakras as, for example, many people associate Christ with the heart chakra. Baha'u'llah taught that the revelations given by the prophets, or messengers of God, which led to the establishment of the great world religions were not all separate, but were connected and progressive through history. They came to certain peoples at certain times and acted as a civilising force for each particular people, the way Mohammed unified and brought great civilisation to the warring tribes of Arabia. This was common sense to me, there can only be one source of creation from which all revelation emanates, and that is the One God.

Only in the last few decades have we been able to see the small planet we inhabit as a whole, and it is easy to forget that in the past different continents, different countries, different cities even, must have seemed like different planets. Through history the One has come to different peoples and been conceived in many different forms and called by as many different names: Yahweh, Jehovah, Allah, Tao, Brahman, Buddha, Baha'u'llah to name but a very few, and there will be followers of each one of those who will stand up indignantly and say, 'How dare you compare my god to that god!' or, 'How dare you refer to so and so as God!' And that's how the fights have started.

> *Knowledge is one point which the ignorant have multiplied!*
> *Hadith of Mohammed*

Religious revelation by the prophets brought codes of laws and ethics which have helped bind peoples together, this is part of the cohesive force of religion. Religion, *re-ligare*, to bind back. In essence religion is nothing to do with names or concepts, it is merely the phenomena of reunification. The laws were often very strict, but perhaps that was what was needed to bind a particular people together at a particular time. The laws that the prophets and messengers have revealed to their peoples have always varied, but behind the different language and idiom in which each spoke, the spiritual teachings remain remarkably similar. However, it is not surprising that when the people from one system met those from another system with their different words and symbols, they seemed like aliens to each other and there was a consequent clash of cultures.

The argument against religion is always that it has

caused great bloodshed and disunity. However, I wonder how much more bloodshed there might have been had there been no religion, and would the body of mankind have made it this far at all? It is what man has done in the name of religion that is the problem. When the Yahweh team met the Christ team the high priests shouted, 'Your god is not our god, you are not the Messiah, crucify him!' When the Christ team met the Mohammed team there were great clashes of swords and self righteous cries of 'Heathens!' and from the other side, 'There is only One God, He is our God and His name is Allah!' But explore the Koran and it is clear that there is no real conflict between Christians and Moslems, the god seems to be the same god.

Religious exclusivity was always a good excuse for a fight, and a good excuse to conquer other territories to make a particular nation rich, but this would probably have happened anyway without the religion, and perhaps the affairs of men would have been even more barbaric. This is not to say there have not been periods of deep abuse by power hungry people doing dreadful things in the name of their religion.

However, the core of good in the religions themselves was always an agent of cohesion in the rising civilisations of Judaism, Christianity, Islam, Buddhism, and Hinduism, and it perhaps acted as a restrainer to those power hungry people within those faiths who may have otherwise abused their power yet more. This common core of good enabled the emergence of scientific progress, social conscience, tolerance, hope, and progressive peace. I think it would help if we read our scriptures more liberally and less literally.

The central nervous system of the human body is the spine and the brain, and it bears an uncanny resemblance to a snake. The Indian tradition of Yoga has seven main centres along the system which they see as wheels spinning with physical and spiritual energies. Working up from the rectum to the crown of the head these centres relate to man's progress from animal instinct to psychological and spiritual awareness, in the same way that mankind's physical evolution is revealed in the development of the human embryo. The chakras form a map that not only illustrates the evolution of consciousness in mankind but also guides the rising consciousness of an individual. When the chakra wheels are spinning and their energies awakened, the life-force itself rises up through the central nervous system and brings the individual into union with God. The Indians call this Kundalini and it is symbolised by the erect cobra.

So, sitting in bed on the Isle of Skye that morning I was wondering about the connection between the chakras of the body of mankind and the founders of the great religions, and how this all might relate to the spiritual maturation of the human race. Then quite suddenly, out of the blue, I was vividly shown the chakras in the body of mankind, and how this might all symbolically fall into place.

The base chakra is Adam, connecting back to the beginning of our evolution, the time of single cells before the one became two. This first man became two as Adam and Eve, the dawning of self-consciousness. He is aboriginal man, nomad man, connected-to-nature wild man. The chakra is red like the raw energy of volcanic lava and is close to the awesome creation of matter. It is the root of instinct and sensation where the autonomic reactions of pure survival arise, fight, freeze, and flight. It defends its territory and its offspring, and it kills to survive.

The second chakra is Abraham. The one who knows the sacred nature of sexuality. It is orange and contains the fire of sexual energy, and is to do with tribe, family, and reproduction of the species. It is the seat of mass thinking and behaviour. The whole story of Abraham is one of genealogy: so-and-so begat so-and-so who begat so-and-so etc., which led to the establishment of the twelve tribes of Israel. He was the archetypal patriarch and father of all nations.

The third chakra is Moses. It is in the solar plexus and is the yellow of the sun. It is where we experience power, passion and emotional response. Moses was the tough kind of man that was needed to lead the Israelites out of servitude in Egypt, through the wilderness back to their homeland. He was abandoned as a baby and left to the hands of fate in a basket on the Nile. The belly is where we feel such things. On his way to his prophet-hood he killed a man and was forgiven by God. The solar plexus is the seat of rooted forgiveness as well as personal power. The laws in his day had to be hard, and he found them set in stone.

The fourth chakra is Christ. It is the green of the fertile earth. It is the heart, and it is the seat of love. The crux/cross of Christ's teachings was love, the Golden Rule, *love thy neighbour as thyself*. He looked back down through the lower chakras and revealed their connectedness to the One when he said, *Before Abraham was, I am*. John 8:58. The three chakras below the heart are to do with Earth: animal, reptile, and raw matter. The three above the heart are to do with Heaven: development of communication, intellect, and spiritual awareness. Christ walked in between Earth and Heaven in the place of the heart, bringing the two together through Love. By his sacrifice, his crucifixion, he broke the heart open and created the channel for the raising of man's mass consciousness toward spirit.

The fifth chakra is Mohammed. It is blue, out of which inspiration speaks. It is at the throat, and is concerned with speech and communication. This is man who can express his knowledge: scientific, rational, inspired, creative man. The bequest of Islam was the development in the Arab world of arithmetic, science and art. Through the clash of cultures Islam infiltrated the Christian world, and there is good cause to suggest that the Renaissance and the Age of Reason was fuelled by the influence of Islam. Even today the black robes of academia pay homage to the Arabic influence.

The sixth chakra is the Bab. It is the third eye, the gateway through which we connect with our spiritual nature. It is the eye through which the mystics see. We are inspired, in-spirited, through our third eye, it is the channel for our intuition, and it wears the indigo robes of spirit. The Bab means *The Gate*, and he was the precursor to Baha'u'llah. He prepared the way for Baha'u'llah just as John the Baptist prepared the way for Christ. This is mystical man, the saint, the poet. The Bab was a mystic who spoke the language of the Sufis (the mystical limb of Islam, of whom Rumi is one of the best known exponents). Like John the Baptist he died young.

His execution was ordered by the Grand Vizier of the Shah of Persia due to pressure from the fanatical Shi'ih clergy, resonating also with the story of the Pharisees and Christ's early death. A short account of the day he died shows the mystery of the man and his death.

On 9th July 1850 the Bab was brought before a firing squad in the barracks square of Tabriz, along with a young follower. When the smoke cleared, the crowd was amazed that the Bab was nowhere to be seen. He was located in the room He had occupied, finishing a conversation with his amanuensis. The commander of the Armenian regiment, Sam Khan, refused to fire a second time and another regiment had to be found. This time their bullets killed the Bab.

From 'A Basic Baha'i Dictionary'

The seventh chakra is Baha'u'llah. It is pure white light, and here one finds union with God. It is the place of transcendence into spirit. This is man as ultimate sage in the wisdom of spirit, mankind in God's image. It is the closest we can get to the Unknowable in manifest form. Baha'u'llah is said to be the culmination of the prophets of God for this age. Just as he completes the cycle started with Adam, he completes the spiritual map of the chakras in the body of mankind. Mankind has come of age in his spiritual evolution, and he now has the wherewithal to grow into full adulthood, and on to the wisdom of old age, the sage, and the worlds beyond death.

I want to emphasise that this was a meditation which sprang out of my own psyche, and it is by no means conventional Baha'i thinking, it is just something which has helped me make sense of things, in a metaphor that is meaningful to me. It is just *one man's opinion of moonlight*, as Donovan sang in the sixties. You might ask, 'Where's Buddha, where's Krishna, where's Lao-Tzu, where's Zoroaster?' Well, the only answer I have is that my psyche is more closely connected to my Judeo-Christian genetic inheritance, and therefore it is natural for my model of understanding to be based on the Semitic tradition, but I have no doubt that they are all in there somewhere. I can only hope that it makes some sense to other people too.

FOURTEEN

The Gateway of Hope

Verily this is the shining morn and the rosy dawn
which will impart unto thee the lights,
and teach thee what thou dost not know
of the facts of the universe.
Thus will the pictures of the supreme world
be printed on the mind.

Abdu'l-Baha

I don't know when this is, though it feels mediaeval. I
am in a deep forest in the heart of old England, surrounded by
beautiful old oaks and other hardwoods, I adore this forest and
I am full of joy. I am astride a strong black stallion, he is my
greatest companion and I know we have been through a lot
together. It has been a long journey so far, and when the forest

293

grows thicker I dismount and rest awhile against a tree, allowing my horse to graze freely. The air is alive with birdsong and the busy humming of insects, and I hear the rustling of the undergrowth as inquisitive animals peek cautiously at us. At peace, I doze.

After my rest, I have to go forward on my own as the forest is too dense for a horse. I leave him there to await my return while I move on towards my destination. I have a golden sabre on my back which I pull out and use to cut my way through the undergrowth, which is soft like ivy. Soon I break through into a beautiful clearing which is protected on all sides by solid walls of tangled undergrowth. From above, shafts of rich copper sunlight filter through the forest canopy. As the foliage closes up behind me I look around feeling warm, safe, and blissfully happy. At the far end of the clearing, built into a darker thicket, I can see a huge portal exquisitely created by nature. It is made up of grasses and heathers decorated with garlands of wild flowers. It is called the Gateway of Hope.

Although I am manifestly alone, I feel anything but alone. All around me I can feel the presence of my ancestors, like a whispering gallery, and they are willing me onward towards the portal. There is a key I have to collect and I know exactly where it is. I walk silently forward, my feet cushioned by layers of fallen leaves. Underneath some leaves to the right of the door I know there is a pit where the key is buried. I clear away the dead leaves above the pit and uncover a large brown-black snake who uncoils herself as soon as she sees me. She knows me, she is an old friend, and I rest my hand on her back, stroking her as she glides off into the undergrowth.

The key is a simple golden triangle which I lift out and polish on my belly. I am blown gently forward towards the door by the breath of my whispering ancestors. I simply touch the door with the key and I am through.

It is dazzling white light, and I feel a great sense of release as there seems to be no gravity. In front of me and all around me I can see all the ancestors who had been beckoning me forward. Amongst them also are all my friends, my past loves, and even my children. I notice Karin and she smiles at me, she knows the part she played for me in my life and for a moment we merge with each other. I see Jessica and all enmity has vanished between us, it is as if we had been merely acting things out for each other in our lives.

I feel very young in this new world, and I am unaccustomed to the overwhelming waves of love coming from all these beings, and tears begin to roll down my cheeks. I become acutely self-conscious of the petty-mindedness and prejudices I bring with me from the other world. Here there is no envy, no bitterness, and no fear between beings, and it is only by the absence of these feelings that I realise what a heavy load they render in the other world. I can be with anyone I want, I can have anything I want, I can do anything I want, and I soon realise that I can go anywhere I want. It is a fantastic feeling of liberation. All these loving beings are there for me, and anything that happened between us in life is forgiven and as such is also forgotten. There is no need to remember troubled lives here, that work is all done.

I realise that I am floating, I feel weightless. There is no pressure either atmospheric or emotional. I keep repeating to myself, 'No pressure, no restrictions, no gravity.' Gravitas is heaviness and seriousness, and it is remarkable how light it feels to be without it. Another strange realisation comes over me as I drift up and away from all the other beings. Because I can have anything I want I no longer have the desire for anything or anyone at all! Since I can have it all, I feel absolutely no need for it. What a glorious feeling of freedom and lightness that brings. I just float in nothingness, as if on a magic carpet. This is no-thing, no-where, yet it is every-thing, every-where.

I realise that knowledge is an earthly thing, but here it is available everywhere and I can tap into it and know anything I want to know, it is written in the ether. But what is organic here, I realise, is wisdom. Here wisdom can still grow.

Slowly I become aware of a presence, and I am floating towards it as if on the gentle current of a calm sea. I am moving on through this realm towards God, and as I get closer wisdom naturally grows. I am moving closer to it without any pressure, any friction or any gravity. The current is love and total willingness.

As I become more aware of my lack of restrictions I think how nice it would be to visit somewhere I love on Earth, and no sooner has the thought crossed my mind than I am there, and I am hovering above the Himalayas. It is a sublime sensation, and I taste the pure air, delicious like nectar, whilst I look down at the jewel that is the Earth. I think to myself, 'Is this why spirit returns to Earth?' What a pleasure this is! And I wonder where I might go next.

I find that I am being drawn somewhere, but I go

willingly without the friction of fear. And I look down on the sun setting upon the endless red ridges of a desert. The desert is crystal clear and sparkles like a gemstone. It is Australia. I hear drumming and the soulful prehistoric drones of the didgeridoo, as I am drawn like a magnet towards the chanting of a group of aborigines around a crackling fire. I realise that they are calling me present and it is a wonderful feeling to be literally drummed up as spirit. These people know I am there, and I know they know, for they are close to spirit and understand how the human connects with spirit. Then it comes clear to me why spirit wishes to enter physical form on Earth: it is in order to experience the wonder of not knowing and of free will, to have the experience of learning things afresh, for this is the one thing that spirit cannot do. So one of the delights of the physical life on Earth is to experience spirit through physical feeling in the weighty gravity of matter, the way that these truly connected aboriginals were doing.

As their ritual comes to a close they release me and I am called back towards the Himalayas. On my way back I look down and see the towering skyscrapers of a big city, and I find it very unattractive, I am repelled by its pollution and its disconnection from me as spirit. I know this is my journey back, for I know that I cannot stay in this future world until I have completed my life on Earth. I remain for a while resting in the blissful air of the Himalayas. In a way it seems stupid to go back, why would any soul be so foolish when it can do anything it wants in the world of spirit? But luckily I have the memory of the beautiful woods, and my horse who no doubt is waiting faithfully for me, and the aborigines who had shown me some of the pleasures that can be had on Planet Earth.

I am aware that re-entry to the Earth life is no different to the perils of a capsule re-entering the Earth's atmosphere from outer space, it has to be done precisely or damage might be done. I return stage by stage, and I must do it of my own volition or I will burn up. I thank the ancestors, friends, and loved ones, and with love they ease my passage back safely through the Gateway.

I put the gold key back in the pit as the friendly snake slides back into her position to guard the key, and I stroke and thank her as she curls up. I rake the leaves back over the pit knowing that I can find it again whenever I want. It is my key and only I know where it is kept. I walk back to the edge of the clearing, part the ivy, and walk out making sure that I close the gap so that only those who have searched can find this place. It occurs to me that the clearing and the Gateway of Hope belong to everybody, but they will only find it if they have searched.

My horse is still there, happily grazing where I left him. Perhaps I have not been gone that long. I take the reins and mount up, still wondering why I came back from that blissful place, and for what reason. But as I ride out through the shimmering English forest I understand that I can be useful in this world, that I have the wherewithal to respond to anything that crosses my path and that the purpose of life is to learn to love, to be of service, and to stay in touch with joy.

I felt wide awake when I drifted out of my body in this way sometime in the summer of 1995. Fact or fantasy, it gave me a confidence in the existence of other realms that I had not had before. Scientists have been saying for years that we only use about ten percent of our brains, and now some are telling us that ninety percent of the universe is missing, and I am wondering if there is a connection between these two facts! What happens to consciousness in a black hole? Could it be possible that the ninety percent of our brain that seems to be inactive is working on another plane in the ninety percent of the universe that is unaccountable? And when we tap into experiences such as I have described here, are we using some of that missing ninety percent? So is what I experienced equally as real as this keyboard that is manifesting out all these words that are appearing in front of me right now? Be that as it may, it was such a relief to get a little perspective on the theatre in which myself and those other protagonists of my life have been taking part. To see Jessica and to simply smile at her and thank her for the experiences she has given me that have driven me forward to find out more about my Self. If only I could always stay in touch with that perspective in this life, but even after all the work I have done, I can still get drawn into all the old fears before I have had time to catch myself.

So, maybe I do have some more work to do whilst my sojourn on this planet lasts, and this is why I had to come back from that blissful place. *Prepare, that ye are received*, as the voice had instructed me all those years ago. It would seem that I have more preparation to do before I am to be received by Death. And, according to my vision at least, meantime I do have in me the capability of resolving everything that crosses my path. I am responsible, I am able to respond.

Heaven knows where we're going, and heaven knows what's

happening to us, was Tolstoy's cry, and who honestly can fathom deeper than that? There are no definitive answers really, only questions.

> *Every answer is a small death, every question a spark of life.*
> John Fowles. 'The Magus'

All Parsifal had to do to heal the Fisher King and bring the spark of life back into his kingdom, was to ask the right question, *Whom does the Grail serve?* What counts in life is not so much right answers as right questions. Questions are raised through experience, both inner and outer. The ability to relate that experience to one's own sense of truth, and to some greater purpose, is to bring that spark of life back to the Grail King, the Self, the God in whose image we are made.

At the end of all his wandering, Goldmund returns to the community of the abbey where he first trained with Narziss as a noviciate monk, and the ageing Narziss is now the abbot. Goldmund has experienced all there is to experience in life: joy, suffering, grief, love, lust, all the extremities of the sensual life. He is now tired and preparing for his death. Each man envies the other. Narziss wonders if it was,

... more valiant, and greater in God's sight, to breast the currents of reality, sin, and accept sin's bitter consequence, instead of standing apart, with well-washed hands, living in sober, quiet security, planting a pretty garden of well-trained thoughts, and walking then, in stainless ignorance, among them - the sheltered beds of a little paradise. It was harder perhaps,

and needed a stouter heart to walk with broken shoes through forest glades, to trudge the roads, suffer rain and snow, want and drought, playing all the games of the senses, and paying for one's losses with much grief.

And Goldmund says to Narziss:

... it seems that you thinkers and theologians can succeed far better than I do in coming to grips with life, and holding despair at arms length. I have long since ceased to envy you your science, my friend, but I envy your calm, your peace, your even temper.

Here is the dilemma I have run across in my life. Is it better to go into the forest alone and cut my own path, or is it better to follow a known path with a community of others, as a candle lighting the way? Is the heroic impulse of the individual dead, or does it flourish as an integral cohesive force in the global community? Joseph Campbell has offered me a glimmering of an answer.

Furthermore, we have not even to risk the adventure alone, for the heroes of all time have gone before us. The labyrinth is thoroughly known. We have only to follow the thread of the hero path, and where we had thought to find abomination, we shall find a god. And where we had thought to slay another, we shall slay ourselves. Where we had thought to travel outward, we will come to the centre of our own existence. And where we had thought to be alone, we will be with all the world.

The Power of Myth

Hesse's book finishes with a fabulous irony. Goldmund has become a skilled craftsman, and in his last days Narziss commissions him to sculpt a new Mother of Christ for the abbey. Finally it is complete and Narziss is invited to see the unveiled figure. Narziss is deeply impressed and recognises that it is the finest image of the Virgin ever to grace his cloisters. But Goldmund says to him,

... Narziss, listen. To shape that figure it needed the whole of my youth, it needed all my vagrancy and loves, and every woman I ever knew.

So this exquisitely moulded figure of the Blessed Virgin was only made possible by Goldmund's secular and sensual life experience with women. What a lovely irony and what a profound truth. Narziss, with his cloistered life and lack of worldly savvy, could never have imagined such a piece. It seems Hesse is saying that it is only through our own experiences of life, consciously integrated, that we can begin to know. Out of the shadows of dark experience comes the light of truth.

Today I think our task is to bring these two worlds together, we must be both Narziss and Goldmund. We must gather the experiences of our lives into the cloisters of our own being. We have to learn to feel again by taking off the armour created by the patriarchy and the age of mechanistic thinking, but without losing reason. We must pay homage to both science and religion.

We live in incredibly neurotic times, what R.D. Laing described as this *appalling state of alienation called normality*, and we need to unravel our neuroses before we can call ourselves truly spiritual. Otherwise how do we know that we are not simply transferring a childish dependence on to a father or a mother whom we call God? Through the integration of the inner work we may become individuated adults, useful parents and elders capable of initiating the young. We must take this into our relationships, our communities, our faiths, and into worldly matters. To do this we have to take some risks, and that might mean making a few mistakes, but I take these mistakes to be only innocent sins, sins committed during an individual's earnest pursuit of his or her own truth.

Mistakes are, after all, the foundations of truth, and if a man does not know what a thing is, it is at least an increase in knowledge if he knows what it is not.

Carl Jung. 'Aion'

FIFTEEN

Quests or answers?

Doubt is a pain too lonely to know
that Faith is his twin brother.

Kahlil Gibran. 'The Prophet'

Conclusions are potentially arid things. For as soon are they are established they can become set in stone, they are the stuff of mindsets and inflexible world-views. It is old spiritual wisdom that one must always be prepared to make a shift and let go of one's attachment to a belief or a system. Conclusions that may have taken years of the shifting sands of inner work and outer experience to arrive at, may require to be released overnight for the sake of an insight towards a greater potential for truth. Holding on to them may only cause inner turmoil and lead to more suffering for ourselves or those around us.

Thus doubt can be seen as a relatively healthy aspect of

the human condition, for it at least implies an open mind. If you are convinced about something, or have a firm belief, then by definition you are closed-minded, you have a world view set in stone.

Quantum physics has shown that all experimentation seems to be subjective, not objective as classical science had taught. In other words the experiment is always effected by the experimenter because they, as part of the whole, are an integral part of the experiment, and therefore have an effect on it. So it is not possible for us to look objectively outside of our own universe, because we are inside of it and an integral part of it. We can only look at what we are already a part of, and thus we are seeing everything subjectively. So if there is a force outside our universe that created all of this, it seems logical that it will always be impossible to observe it objectively. Like an unborn baby in the womb who is part of, but cannot see, its mother, we are inside our universe unable to observe it from the outside; so it is logical to say it may forever remain unknown.

If God is essentially unknowable, as much of the perennial spiritual wisdom tells us, then how can anyone know *the* way, or say 'you can only go *this* way to get to God.' In this sense doubt, uncertainty, and not knowing, is closer to God because God is impossible to know! I think it is only possible to be acquainted with God from the inside, it is an entirely personal experience, a paradox that is almost impossible to put into words. In a sense we cannot know God, we can only *be* God. I cannot be told that there is a God and believe, I can only concede to being a participant in this wide universe and experience God directly and subjectively from within. And this is a condition of being, not of doing, saying, or believing.

> *You can verbalise your knowledge,*
> *and you can know what you're saying*
> *the rest must pass over in silence.*
>
> *Ludwig Wittgenstein*

Monotheism in the hands of mankind can become dangerous and distorted, and has led to all the squabbling over your God versus my God. For although I think it is true to say 'God is One' and 'there is only one God,' it is equally true to say, 'God is everything, and nothing.'

As I stood at the stern of a boat one Spring and stared over sparkling blue waters towards a cherished Greek island shrinking into the distance, I had an insight drop in from the blue. It was simply this, that getting smaller is as infinite as getting larger. It was a nice little brain-teaser, that small is potentially as big as large. If as a premise, one is the sum (interestingly *sum* is the Latin for *I am*) of everything in this universe, and we as human beings stand at say one-eighth within that whole, then if you expand into largeness towards the finite one by doubling up at each step, within three stages you get to one (i.e. eighth to quarter to half to one). However, if you go backwards from an eighth towards zero, halving each time, you actually never reach zero simply because you are halving each time, and theoretically this can go on ad infinitum. As William Blake famously wrote in 'Auguries of Innocence',

To see a World in a Grain of Sand

And a Heaven in a Wild Flower,
Hold Infinity in the palm of your hand
And Eternity in an hour.

Looking out at the stars and beyond nobody knows where, or if, it all ends, and even if it does isn't the no-thing beyond the boundaries of the cosmos potentially some-thing else? It is all very uncertain, unknown and totally mind-boggling. Here we are though, standing on our blue and green jewel of a planet looking out into the black of the stellar night, and at least we can pinch ourselves and know that we exist at the magnitude of the human frame.

With its electron microscopes, its particle accelerators, and all its theories, science sees molecules, atoms, electrons, protons and neutrons, particles, waves, quarks, superstrings, and beyond to who knows what. Our perceptions of time and size can only be a small window into the boundlessness of infinity. So is it not equally credible that the creative force exists in the infinite smallness, as it might in the somewhat dubiously infinite largeness? Thus, for me, does the concept 'God is within' become not only a practical possibility, but a more rational scenario. William Blake again,

Thus man forgot that all gods reside within the human breast.

The creative force, the immanent power of God, is a potential that exists as much in a single atom as in a whole cosmos. This is old wisdom as a Persian mystic's poem relates:

Split the atom's heart, and lo!
Within it thou wilt find a sun
          Quoted by Baha'u'llah in 'The Seven Valleys'

I feel I carry God within me, I feel that I emanate from God. I have become reluctant to call myself anything any more, and I am no longer certain how to play it in the outside world other than to follow my own thread, and to obey my own truth. Doubt about a definitive outer path has been eating away at me for years, and recently I have had to act on the call I have been hearing within me that asks me to cut my own path through the forest.

For me, one of the most precious principles of the Baha'i faith is to pursue an *unfettered independent investigation into the truth,* and it is perhaps ironic that my own quest has led me to pull back from the outer form of the Faith for now. It had been with me during a very difficult and traumatic nine years, it had been the Virgil who had generously escorted me on my journey through the Inferno. I feel that I have internalised the Faith and I continue to walk with it towards the Beloved. The form of the beautiful young Karin, my Beatrice, stands before me like a glorious phantom, beckoning me onwards to what I pray is Paradiso!

Nine and nineteen are the mystic numbers of the Baha'i faith, they symbolise wholeness and fullness, the completion of a cycle; for nine moves on to ten which is to return to one again, and the beginning of a new cycle.

It had been a long struggle for me to decide to pull back from the Faith, and it all came to a head for me on the

309

morning of April 19th 1996. I was meditating on the number nine and the fact that it must be roughly nine years since I stumbled across this Faith. I decided to look back in my journals to see when exactly it had all begun, only to find that it was on April 19th 1987 that serendipity had taken me to the meeting with Gloria Feizi and the Lotus Temple in the suburbs of Delhi. It was precisely nine years ago to the very day. So it seemed that the wheel had indeed come full circle, and that I had arrived back where it had all started, and that now I knew the place for the first time.

And this book is its first fruits.

I sat down and wrote a letter of explanation to my friends in the Faith, and in it I quoted Abdu'l-Baha's beautiful words that a fellow pilgrim had written down for me during my visit to Haifa in 1988.

At the gate of the garden, some stand and look within, but do not enter.
Others step inside, behold its beauty, but do not penetrate far.
Still others, encircle this garden, inhaling the fragrance of the flowers,
and having enjoyed its full beauty, pass out again by the same gate.
But there are always some who enter and,
becoming intoxicated with the splendour of what they behold,
remain for life to tend the garden.

Abdu'l-Baha makes no judgments on who chooses to do what, and for now I was one of those passing out again by the same gate *having enjoyed its full beauty*, feeling confident that I was moving forward on my journey with his blessing. He stated Baha'i is *a movement, not an organization,* and this makes so much sense to me. Movement implies vibration and change, the true nature of life. Organisation is necessary in human affairs, but it is secondary to the thing that moves it. I feel that every prophet of God that has birthed on to this planet, has rested his finger on the ground and has earthed a new and higher energy. This quickening vibrates into every atom of our cosmos, residing implicately in every form of life and every material thing. Its resonance yields a potential for yet higher consciousness, which can be revealed through man in particular, but is exclusive to no man, and to no particular creed.

And it is because I still believe that Baha'u'llah is a manifestation of God for this age, that as far as the Faith is concerned I am still a Baha'i. It is generous, inclusive and ultimately liberating, putting no pressure on me to be either in or out, or anything other than I feel. I feel free to be or not to be. I am and yet I am not, I am not and yet I am. This is the kind of paradoxical conclusion that would make all the gurus I have ever met in my life very proud of me I'm sure!

'Have you also learned that secret from the river; that there is no such thing as time?'

A bright smile spread over Vasudeva's face.

'Yes, Siddhartha,' he said. 'Is this what you mean? That the river is everywhere at the same time, at the source and at the mouth, at the waterfall, at the ferry, at the current, in the ocean and in the mountains, everywhere, and that the present only exists for it, not the shadow of the

past, nor the shadow of the future?'

'That is it,' said Siddhartha, 'and when I learned that, I reviewed my life and it was also a river, and Siddhartha the boy, Siddhartha the mature man and Siddhartha the old man were only separated by shadows, not through reality. Siddhartha's previous lives were also not in the past, and his death and his return to Brahma are not in the future. Nothing was, nothing will be, everything has reality and presence.'

Siddhartha spoke with delight. This discovery had made him very happy. Was then not all sorrow in time, all self-torment and fear in time? Were not all difficulties and evil in the world conquered as soon as one conquered time, as soon as one dispelled time? He had spoken with delight, but Vasudeva just smiled radiantly at him and nodded his agreement.

Hermann Hesse. 'Siddhartha'

At the end of his journey Siddhartha finds the essence (from *esse*, to be), and he lives in simplicity beside the river, resonant with the Aum. He is the ferryman who helps journeying pilgrims to and fro across the waters between the two lands that represent the material and spiritual worlds. Perhaps that is all we can ask of this life, to find our purpose and our place, and to be of simple service to others on their quests.

Like the songlines which guide aborigines across their country and across their history, I believe that we each enter this world with a resonance in our heart that will make us feel at home in this world. Every one of our melodies is unique, and if we give ourselves the time to listen, out of the silence we may catch the song of the nightingale that is perched on the

Tree of Life rooted in our breast. Once we hear it, we can resonate to it and bring our lives into harmony with it. The song springs from the pulsating source of the original heartbeat, the Aum, and is the golden strand that can lead us onward to our destination. The song *is* the purpose, and to be aligned with this purpose is to be living authentically. We write life as life writes us, and we are the author of the dream that is dreaming us, on Earth as it is in Heaven.

Me, when I hear my song, my heart is full to overflowing and I feel like a troubadour.

ABOUT THE AUTHOR

Nick Price was born in Oxford, England, in 1951. He was sent away to boarding schools from the age of seven. At leaving age his housemaster, for career advice, suggested he would make a good psychologist or detective as he seemed to understand people so well. However, as a child of the sixties, he was determined to become a successful photographer instead. This lasted about twenty years until his marriage disintegrated and things began to fall apart. Consequently, in his search to make sense of it all, he retrained with Elisabeth Kübler-Ross in her Life, Death, and Transition bereavement work, and subsequently as a Biodynamic body-oriented psychotherapist with Gerda Boyesen. Since then, his therapeutic group work has taken him to all kinds of nooks and crannies around the world. His housemaster was right after all.

Printed in Poland
by Amazon Fulfillment
Poland Sp. z o.o., Wrocław